LOGAN'S WIFE

Minita Sype Brown
and
Rosalie Hunt Mellor

Review and Herald® Publishing Association
Washington, DC 20039-0555
Hagerstown, MD 21740

This book was
Edited by Gerald Wheeler
Designed by Bill Kirstein
Cover Art by Joe Van Severan
Type set: 11 pt. Times Roman

PRINTED IN U.S.A.

R&H Cataloging Service
Sype-Brown, Minita, 1921-1988
Logan's wife, by Minita Sype-Brown and Rosalie Hunt Mellor.

1. Sype, Minnie (Day), 1869-1956. I. Mellor, Rosalie Hunt, 1920- joint author. II. Title.
[B]

ISBN 0-8280-0508-7

CHAPTER 1

Home Missions

When Minnie had started out that morning her resolves had been firm and fearless. But now, sitting in the wagon beside her husband, Logan, eyes fixed on the powerful hind quarters of Blackie and Nell, she wished she were back home baking bread.

It had all seemed so simple and easy then when she had handed up her bag of magazines for him to set beside the butter and eggs. But now, as the wagon drew closer and closer to the fringe of houses scattered along the way to town, doubts and fears nibbled at her.

Turning to her husband with a depreciating little laugh, she said, "I don't think I'll stop today. I'll just ride on along to town with you. The wind is coming up and—" She drew her coat up around her throat and settled back in the rough seat, bracing her feet against the jolts.

Her husband gave no sign that he heard her, and when they came to a house partly hidden by bushes and trees, he halted the team. "What's wrong, Logan? Why are you stopping here?" she asked, turning a puzzled face toward him.

"You want to sell magazines, don't you? You said you were going to stop at every house on the way to town. Here is the first house. Go ahead."

"But Logan, this house is—is—look at it!" Her eyes traveled the crooked path leading up to a house that huddled, gray and forlorn, some distance from the road. Two uncurtained windows stared emptily out at the yard where a tethered cow grazed.

"Somebody lives here, Minnie. Maybe somebody who wants

and needs one of your magazines. Go on.'' When she didn't move, he added, ''It will be good experience for you.''

Slowly she climbed down and picked her way up the long rutted trail that led to the house. Balancing herself on the plank that served as a stoop, she stared at the bleak, unfriendly door before knocking. The thought ran through her mind that has comforted timid salesmen through the ages—*I hope there is nobody at home*. Getting no answer, she rapped again, louder this time, but no sound came from the dark rooms. With a sigh of relief she started to leave when she heard a stirring on the other side of the door, a disquieting rustle growing louder as if something were being dragged across the floor.

Just as she was about to flee, the door opened, screeching in protest. A tall, gaunt man stood there, his face bitter and unshaven. Leaning against a home-made crutch for support, he had trouble focusing his red-rimmed eyes on his visitor. The reek of alcohol hung about him and bottles littered the room beyond and lay scattered around the yard.

''I—I don't suppose you would like to buy a paper, sir?'' she stammered when she could find her voice.

He bent unsteadily forward and spat a stream of tobacco juice expertly between his teeth before shouting in slurred tones, ''No, I don't want no paper!'' and slammed the door so hard the frail house shook.

Minnie ran down the twisting trail and out to the wagon where she startled Logan by leaping up to the seat and throwing her sack of magazines at his feet. ''That is the last time I am going to try to sell anything to anyone.''

''What on earth happened?''

''A terrible man yelled at me and slammed the door. He was drunk and ugly—and I am never going up to another house again, ever.''

''You aren't going to quit after one try, are you? There are people out there waiting for Christian literature. And not all of them will be drunk. You've been planning to sell magazines for weeks.''

''But I didn't think it would be like this,'' she said, blinking back the tears. ''I thought some nice lady would come to the door and invite me in and we would talk.''

''That nice lady is out there waiting for you,'' he assured her.

''Easy for you to say.'' Her mouth began to set in a way he knew well.

"Are you going to throw all of your hopes and plans away just because of one disagreeable drunk? You know what happens when a man gets thrown from a horse. They say if he doesn't get right back on, he may never ride again. Therefore, you must go up to the next house."

When her husband halted the wagon in front of a neat bungalow, she climbed down and walked to the door. No one answered, but her courage growing, she went up to the neighboring place where two big dogs ran out barking savagely. A red-faced woman, surly and loud, rushed out to call them off.

When Minnie asked if she would like to buy a Christian magazine, she shrilled, "No, I ain't got no time to read and no money to buy papers. It's just work, work, work around here, what with six kids and my man gone all the time." She closed the door, her loud, complaining voice growing fainter as Minnie walked away.

Further on three little boys playing out by the road disappeared like a covey of quail when they caught sight of the wagon, but a young mother stood in the doorway and waved a greeting. Pushing lank strings of hair back from her thin face, she peeled two wide-eyed children from her leg before she asked Minnie in. "These young'uns is just like wild animals," she explained. "We just moved here and they never see no one they know."

She was eager to get something to read and to talk with another woman. Buying a *Signs of the Times*, she made her visitor promise that she would come back.

From then on Minnie organized her week so that she could set aside Thursdays for witnessing visits. Since it was the day Logan took the butter and eggs to town and bought supplies, she often went with him to sell magazines. If the weather was bad and she couldn't get out, she wrote letters, made sunbonnets to sell, or did sewing for others so as to raise money to carry on her witnessing projects. She made quilts for missions and when company came, she had quilt blocks handy to work on while visiting.

Near the kitchen door she stocked a reading rack so that she could give any tramp, salesman, or caller of any kind a magazine or a tract.

In those days late in the 1800s tramps traveled about the country, homeless men hitching rides on freight trains and wandering from place to place begging for food and looking for a barn or a haystack where they could spend the night. One morning Minnie heard something shuffling around up in the haymow when she went out to milk. It was just light enough in the barn to see without a lantern as she set the milking stool down, pressed her head against the warm flank of the cow, and began squirting milk into the pail. As the first tinny sound deepened into a deep swoosh, swoosh, the smell of warm milk filled the barn, and she heard more footsteps, heavy now, up in the haymow. Bits of hay and chaff floated down. "Hello," she called out, "who is shaking hay into the milk?"

The two tramps who climbed down from the steep ladder that led to the loft were dressed in once splendid suits, now threadbare and covered with hay which they tried in vain to brush off. They stood there like a comedy team about to go into a dance. Minnie remembered them both, Boxcar Willie with his good-natured, toothless grin and his partner, Tennessee, so shy he pulled his hat down over his face to cover his eyes. The latter hunched inside a coat that had once belonged to a well-fed banker.

"Mornin' Ma'am," Boxcar Willie greeted her. "The milk smelled so good we was wondering if we could have some." Each man held a tin can which she filled.

"Come on up to the back door now," she said. "I have some reading for you to take along." At the back door she set the foaming pail down and handed them each a tract. "Mind you read it now. You know God loves you."

"Yes, Ma'am. Thank you, Ma'am." And they headed toward the railroad tracks to hop another freight train. She never knew if they read the publications or not. Her neighbor said they just lined their shoes with them.

Minnie became a familiar figure in the community as she sold magazines and gave away tracts. She spent her nights studying and her days witnessing, and as the seasons progressed, so did her enthusiasm. As April moved into May and she saw the pale burst of blossoming trees along the way, it was like a sign of Christ's coming to her.

All through that summer she visited and wrote letters, enclosing a tract or a poem after first praying that God would impress her to send the right thing for each individual. One woman answered her letter and said she had been at the point of giving up her Christian life, but when she read the poem Minnie had enclosed, she got down on her knees and rededicated her life to God. Another wrote that she had begun observing the Sabbath after reading the tract in her letter.

CHAPTER

2

The Singing Master

Back when she was 19, Minnie had gone to Sand Creek Township to teach school, and there she had met the singing master. She had begun hearing about Logan Sype as soon as she arrived at her boarding place in Union County, Iowa. He seemed to be the kind of man who was always on people's minds. His name kept coming up in every conversation. At the first quilting bee she attended the girls began a prolonged tittering as soon as they heard his name, and they quickly lapsed into hushed discussion and laughter.

Millicent Defoe cast a disapproving look at them and said rather sourly in an aside to Myra Olds, "Giggle all they want to, he has escaped them for 32 years."

"Humph," Myra had sniffed, "who else would starch those white shirts like that but his mamma."

Overhearing them, one of the younger women commented, "Well, you have to admit he is charming."

"And good looking," put in another.

At that Myra Olds tapped her hand, the one with the thimble, against the quilting frame and offered sharply, "Well, if you ask me, handsome is as handsome does."

"He doesn't smoke, you know."

"But that funny religion of his."

"Well, anyway, I like to see him drive past in that fancy buggy."

"And don't you just love to hear him sing!"

There came another tap from Myra Olds' thimble then, this time on her scissors, and a tart "Did we come here to quilt or to talk about Logan Sype?"

Later at a church supper Minnie had heard two of the men discussing him in low tones over their pie and coffee. "Can't seem to quite make a go of it," said one.

"Seems like he can't get along with his dad and can't get along without him."

For weeks Logan Sype was everywhere but nowhere, heard of but never seen, and Minnie felt a growing curiosity about him. The mystery around him annoyed her, for she was not one to play games, but the enigma lingered until early in October when the Sand Creek School scheduled a song fest, and Logan Sype would be the singing master.

Her feelings were mixed as she got ready that Saturday night. She was prepared to dislike the singing master but found herself arranging her hair with special care and pressing her best dress. Nor did she have to have someone tell her who the singing master was. In a room crowded with women in calico dresses and men in clean overalls, he stood out, the only young man in a navy suit and sparkling white shirt. He had combed his dark hair sleekly back to one side, and his face was lean and dark and serious except when he smiled—which was often. Not tall, he stood extremely straight as short men often do.

When he saw her he immediately approached her, walking with quick, nervous steps. Bending forward slightly, he said, "You must be Miss Day. I am Logan Sype."

So this is Logan Sype, she thought to herself as she watched him leading the songfest, clearly enjoying it. In spite of her reservations, she felt his warmth and found it flattering when he lingered afterwards to talk.

In the middle of that week he stopped at the schoolhouse where she was busy checking papers and asked her to go to a lecture in Afton. That fall and winter they went to social events and took long drives out in the country in the fancy buggy she had heard so much about.

One day as they rode slowly along a wooded road he began telling her about his family. Five brothers of Pennsylvania Dutch origin had migrated to America about 1690 from the Rhineland in Germany and settled in Pennsylvania. They moved on west to Ohio.

"They are all go-getters," he said. "My uncle runs Sype's

Mercantile, you know, and as for my father, he is a real farmer. All of them are successful—not like me—I—" and his face clouded as he looked away. Then with a shrug he said quickly, "Did you know one of my ancestors was an Indian chief?"

"That's why you are dark complexioned. I thought maybe you were Spanish."

"No, Indian. Chief John Logan was my great-great-grandfather. My grandfather, John Sype, one of the five brothers, married Mary, the daughter of Chief John Logan. Logan's mother was a Cayuga Indian and his father was a Frenchman. Chief John Logan lived peacefully with the white man until a band of renegade whites slaughtered his family. This pushed him over the edge and he went out for revenge, and he himself became a killer, taking scalps until he had 30 on his tribal belt.

"He gave a speech one time which someone wrote down. Here, I have a copy of it." Logan fished around in his pocket and brought out a piece of paper carefully folded inside an envelope.

Reining the horse to a stop, he said, "Let me read this to you:

" 'I appeal to any white man to say if he ever entered Logan's cabin hungry and he gave him not meat; if he ever came cold and naked and he clothed him not. During the course of the last long and bloody war, Logan remained idle in his cabin, an advocate for peace.

" 'Such was my love for the whites that my countrymen pointed as I passed and said, "Logan is a friend of the white man." I had even thought to have lived with you but for the injuries of one man, Colonel Cresap, the last spring in cold blood and unprovoked, murdered the relatives of Logan, not even sparing wives and children. There runs not a drop of my blood in the veins of any living creature.

" 'This called on me for revenge. I have sought it. I have killed many. I have fully glutted my vengeance. For my country I rejoice in the beams of peace; but do not harbor a thought that mine is a joy of fear. Logan never felt fear. He will not turn on his heel to save his life. Who is there to mourn for Logan? Not one.' "

"How sad," she commented. "Whatever happened to him?"

"It is thought that he married a Shawnee Indian woman after the massacre.'' He took Minnie's hand in his and continued, ''He is a real hero to me. He really took charge of things. That same blood flows in my veins. After all, he was my great-great-grandfather. Someday I am going to take a stand, amount to something.''

When he continued to hold her hand, gazing dreamily off into the distance, she thought he was going to say something else, but he didn't. Instead he tucked the robe around her, picked up the lines, and started the horse toward home.

The strange unsettling courtship went on into the winter. He continued to call on her, sometimes coming several times a week, and then vanishing for days without so much as a note. At the Sand Creek box social, he bid on her box so he could eat with her, but then she didn't see him for three weeks. Rumors flew that his business had failed, that he had quarreled with his father, that he was leaving the country.

The ribbing and teasing she got from the girls was not always good natured. Logan had long been an object of interest to the local gossips and they did not overlook her relationship with him. No ladies' meeting was complete without someone asking a question intended to stir up a discussion about their relationship.

''How is the on-again, off-again romance coming along?'' her neighbor Beatrice inquired.

Tempted to tell her it was none of her business, Minnie managed to say dryly, ''Off-again more than on-again.''

''Speaking of dates, Minnie, have you set one yet?'' Millicent Defoe asked, peering over her wire-rimmed spectacles, her long thin nose and slit of a mouth reminding Minnie of an old hen.

''If I do,'' she replied with cloying sweetness, ''you'll be the first to know, Milly. In fact, you'll probably know before I do. Be sure and tell me so I can get a proper gown.''

All of it left Minnie furious and her replies were often sarcastic. Ever since childhood she had been impatient and high-tempered. It was something she had to fight all of her life.

As Minnie worked at school one day Logan drove up after a long absence, splashing through the puddles from the thawing February snows. Running up the steps, he knocked smartly and called out, ''Anybody home?''

''Hello, stranger,'' she greeted him, checking a biting remark. ''Are you lost?''

''Minnie,'' he said, walking eagerly toward her. ''It has been a while, hasn't it? You see, I was having some business problems, but that's all in the past now. I have rented a farm and it is doing well. But I stopped to see if you would go to a meeting with me tonight in Afton. I want you to hear this preacher. Please, Minnie. It will be a beautiful night for a drive."

He was hard to resist and she liked him and enjoyed being with him. In fact, the only thing she saw standing between them was his religion. She herself went to the Christian Church and he was a Seventh-day Adventist. To her thinking his religion was a bit strange, but it impressed her that he didn't use tobacco. Long ago she had decided that no young man would ever puff tobacco smoke in her face.

Nervous and excited as she got ready that night, she pulled on her best black taffeta dress and swept her dark hair high on her head. Pinching her full cheeks to make them look redder, she studied the round face in the mirror. Did he really like her? When he helped her up into the buggy and pulled the buffalo robe around her with special tenderness, she thought to herself that surely he liked her—at least a little.

Logan led the singing for the meeting, his rich voice a musical touchstone for the others. Minnie studied the lean face with the smiling light brown eyes that sought her own when they all sang "I love thee, I love thee, I love thee, my Lord." Confused then, she dropped her eyes and tried to straighten out the tangled thoughts that raced through her head. She dreamed of more for her and Logan than songfests and rides in his fancy buggy. That winter she had been bridesmaid for two of her friends, and she wondered if that was as close as she was ever going to come to the altar.

Then something happened to change everything. One could hardly call it spring yet, for the air was like ice with snow piled in hard packed drifts, and no one had seen a robin. But on one of those sunny days when the cardinals fly to the top of the highest tree and whistle that loud, sweet song so hope stirs that spring is on the way, Anton Harrison came to town.

Not only was he from Des Moines, bringing with him a city sophistication, but he was a handsome young man, and when he bought the hardware store, it seemed that every family in town had suddenly run out of nails and young women demanded to run the errand to replenish the supply. Tall, self-assured, and somewhat of a flirt, he began at once to court the local girls, going from one to another.

Logan watched him with some amusement until one night at a social Anton Harrison began paying special attention to Minnie. He sat by her and brought cider and donuts to her and when it came time to leave, he asked to take her home. When she explained that she had come with Logan, Anton Harrison took her hand in his and with a meaningful look murmured in a low voice intended for her ears alone, but overheard by Logan anyway, "Another time then, my dear, good evening."

That night on the way home Logan stopped the buggy, took her in his arms, told her he could not live without her, and asked her to marry him.

CHAPTER

3

The Sabbath

At first the difference in religion did not seem to be of great importance. Long before the wedding she had told him, "You know that I belong to the Christian Church and that I plan to continue going there where my friends are. It is a warm, comfortable place to worship. And to tell the truth, I am satisfied with my beliefs and have no intention of changing my religion."

"I don't expect you to change for me, Minnie. I want you to do what *you* have to do in *your* own search for truth. You keep on going to your church and I'll go to mine."

"But it would be nice to go to church together sometimes. You will go with me at least on Easter and Christmas, won't you?"

"Better than that," he promised. "I'll go with you every Sunday if you'll attend my church every Saturday."

So they settled the matter of religion, were married on March 6, 1889, and started housekeeping on the farm that Logan had rented near Afton. While they disagreed on some things, they both believed that they should have a Christian home. Every morning they had Bible reading and prayer and each Saturday and Sunday dressed up and went to church.

This isn't right, she told herself some time later. *When I keep both days I am keeping neither. Only one can be the Holy Sabbath. I might as well not observe either.* She studied the issue of the Sabbath secretly, for she believed that she and the majority of Christians were honoring the day that God had set aside for worship for Christianity, and she hoped to win her husband over to that fact.

After wrestling with the dilemma by herself and finding no answers as to why the Sabbath had changed from Saturday to Sunday, she didn't know which way to turn. Suddenly the answer came to her as if someone had written it in the heavens. Jamming her hat on her head, she burst out the door and headed down the road toward town. She would go to her pastor and he would explain everything.

Pastor Burns ushered Minnie into his study. Although she had married "that Advent," she had remained a good member of the Christian Church, but he worried about her, fearing that she might wander into perdition by dallying with other doctrines.

In his study she looked across the desk at the thin, aesthetic face with the white hair and sideburns, the unmistakable quality of elegance that hung about him. She relaxed and thought here at last was someone who could make sense out of her perplexing problem. The conversation began politely, but Minnie could not wait. She blurted out, "What I really came for, Pastor, was about the Sabbath question."

Sitting behind his desk and putting his hands together in a prayerful pose, Pastor Burns replied, "Question, Mrs. Sype? What question do you mean?"

"You know, Pastor. Why does everyone keep Sunday holy instead of Saturday?"

Leaning forward with a benign smile, he said, "Why, my dear, Sunday is the Lord's day."

"What do you mean by 'the Lord's day'?"

"Our Lord rose from the dead on that day after the crucifixion. Surely you know that." The carefully modulated voice began to reveal a hint of irritation.

"Yes," Minnie persisted, "but where in the Bible does it say that for that reason or any other reason the Sabbath was changed?"

A frown crossed the austere face as he opened a gilt-edged Bible on his desk and turned the pages. The pale hands lifted above the thin leaves like hovering birds and then paused. "Here we are, Mrs. Sype, right here in Revelation 1:10 it reads: 'I was in the spirit on the Lord's day—' "

"But it doesn't say which day the Lord's day was," she objected, but he ignored her remark, closed the Bible, and stood, bringing the interview to a close.

Then in a lofty tone he said, "Only Jews keep Sabbath anymore, my dear. That old law was done away with long ago.''

Angered at his patronizing manner and not trusting herself to speak, she left without another word. Now more confused than ever, she made her way home in deep thought, her mind turning the problem around and around. It troubled her for weeks although she and Logan continued to attend church on both days.

Then one morning after Logan had left early to work in the fields, she ran down the road the short distance to her father-in-law's house. Minnie knew that James Sype had been elder of the Afton Seventh-day Adventist Church for years and that he studied the Bible with both zeal and joy. He had accumulated the only private library in the county and had a reputation as a great reader and student. She would ask him about the Sabbath.

Without knocking she burst into the kitchen where the smell of pancakes filled the room and made her remember she hadn't eaten that morning. James, who was buttering a stack, looked up in surprise as the door opened. The cakes were piled one on top of another and were brown and crisp around the edges with a tantalizing curl of steam rising as the butter melted into the little holes.

Minnie flung herself into a chair at the table and before she could speak her mother-in-law, Harriet, placed a stack of steaming cakes before her. ''Here now, I bet you haven't had breakfast.''

For the moment Minnie forgot why she had come as she buttered her pancakes and began to eat. ''Delicious,'' she said, holding a piece up and looking at it intently. ''And so light. I don't see how you do it, Mother Sype. Mine don't turn out this way.''

Harriet put another cake on her plate, saying, ''Buttermilk. I make them with buttermilk. It makes the difference.''

''But I didn't really come for breakfast,'' her daughter-in-law said, turning toward Mr. Sype. ''Something is driving me out of my mind, Father. Will you please explain the Sabbath to me?''

James Sype slowly poured syrup on his pancakes as he said, ''The Sabbath has been precious to me ever since I discovered it.''

''How did you learn about it?''

''By studying the Bible. I started to observe the Sabbath before I knew anyone else was keeping it.''

''Really? What courage you had.''

''It is hard to be different,'' he admitted. ''People look at you and point you out, and, I suppose, talk about you. But I kept the Sabbath by myself for a long time and then Harriet joined me and, of course, the children. Then one day I heard of a group of Sabbath-keepers, the Seventh-day Adventists, so I joined them. That was about 1860, three years before the organization of the General Conference."

"But what convinced you at the beginning when you first read about it?"

"I went from one Bible text to another, and it began to take shape until it was clear as day. It was like the Lord speaking to me."

"But why is it so important?" She sighed. "Why does it matter? After all, what does it have to do with your faith?"

"The Sabbath, you must realize, is a memorial of God's creation. For six days He worked and created and on the seventh He rested. We acknowledge His creation when we observe the Sabbath. God made the Sabbath, man made the false Sabbath," he concluded.

Sitting in the warm kitchen they studied around the table as they finished the hot cakes and then long afterwards. When Minnie walked slowly home, she looked at God's nature with a different perspective.

The following Sabbath as she attended the small church with Logan, it seemed as if the minister preached directly to her. His sermon had as its text Matthew 7:13 and 14: "Enter ye in at the strait gate for wide is the gate, and broad is the way that leadeth to destruction, and many there be which go in thereat. Because strait is the gate and narrow is the way which leadeth unto life, and few there be that find it."

Looking around at the few worshiping on that Sabbath day at the small, humble church with its hand-hewn pews, she slid closer to Logan, and he covered her hand with his.

"The wide gate," she mused as the congregation stood to sing. "I have been entering the wide gate with the many on Sunday. Now I must leave the larger group and worship with the few who are entering the strait gate."

She felt a turning in her life then and the next Sunday she told Logan he could go out to the fields, for they wouldn't be attending church that day. Putting on her house dress, she began to clean and bake as if it were any other day, but she had a strange feeling that things were not right, that she should not be working but should be getting ready for church.

That Sunday morning the bell in the old steeple of the Christian Church pealed forth, the solemn tones calling everyone to worship.

Hearing the bell ring, she felt a great loss and sadness. As her friends went by on their way to church, she stood at the window with tears in her eyes.

One by one, by twos and threes they passed. Her old friend Samanda drove by with someone Minnie didn't know, a stranger in her buggy. The Carlson sisters had new hats. Gazing after her friends now going one way and she another, she had never felt so forlorn and forsaken. They seemed to be walking out of her life forever that Sunday morning, and she stood behind the curtain and sobbed as they vanished around a turn in the road.

"Do You ask this of me?" she cried out to God.

She turned then and walked into the sitting room with her Bible in hand, knelt down in prayer, and said in her direct way, "Lord, this question of the Sabbath must be settled forever. You know I do not want to be separated from my friends, but I realize that they can never save me. I must take Your word as my guide."

All alone there with the memory of her friends moving in a steady line out of her life, she turned to the Ten Commandments and studied them over carefully. Then she said, "I can never be a Christian and knowingly break one of these commandments. The fourth commandment says, 'The seventh day is the Sabbath of the Lord thy God.' " She vowed that from that day on she would observe the Sabbath of the Lord.

In July 1889, Minnie joined the Seventh-day Adventist Church. The Bible became a new book to her and she spent more and more time studying it. Busy as she was with her housework and the tasks on the farm, she still found time to search the Holy Word. Even when she washed dishes, she had the Bible propped up before her so she could memorize texts of Scripture as she worked. James Sype often came over after supper and he and Minnie studied the Bible together—often until twelve o'clock at night.

CHAPTER

4

Let Your Light So Shine

"How I would like to share this with others," Minnie told herself as she stared at a passage with growing wonder. Then the eagerness faded from her face as she added, "But I am just a woman and not a preacher."

"But, Minnie," her father-in-law had encouraged, "who knows what a handmaiden of the Lord can do?"

She and James had been studying the book of Revelation, and he pointed out the prophecy of the rise of the United States in the thirteenth chapter. One morning later that same month as she read the Bible alone she came upon a passage that would change her life.

The words in Matthew 5—"Let your light so shine"—jumped out at her from the page, and when she read in the seventh chapter, "Ye shall know them by their fruits," she knew she must spread the gospel. She could keep it to herself no longer. Now she must go out and share it with others.

Reading further she found where Peter told the centurion that Christ went about witnessing and had commanded His followers to do the same. The thought kept gnawing at her mind as she went about her work, and although she saw herself as only a single individual, the sense of calling persisted. *What can I do? How can I witness?* Such questions haunted her mind night and day.

The answer came to her one evening in April when she went out to shut the chicken house door for the night The air was cool and smelled faintly like water. A farm dog barked from the valley beyond and another answered farther away, the sound made faint by distance. Black twigs were etched against the silver-colored sky that grew darker from west to east. The evening star hung low, brighter than she had ever remembered, and it was at that moment that it came to her that the best way to witness was through the printed word.

That week she began selling papers and giving away tracts on Thursdays when Logan took the butter and eggs to town. The more she worked, the more she felt convinced that she must devote her life to Christian witnessing.

Now she went out every week to witness, and even though she had two small children by then, she didn't neglect her missionary activities. With her two little boys, Ross and Jimmy, she became a familiar sight going from door to door with magazines and other publications.

When the circus came to town that summer she had her first experience working in a big crowd. She had never attended a circus before and wouldn't have gone to this one if it hadn't been for Ross. The two little boys, in town with their father, saw the circus posters in Sype's Mercantile. With their heads filled with the circus, they ran back to the wagon where their father waited, and shouted the news. "Pa, Pa, a circus is coming to town!"

Logan stared impassively as the boys climbed up the spokes of the wagon wheel into the wagon bed where Ross clutched his father's arm, pleading, "Can we go, can we, Pa, huh?"

"Nope," came the laconic reply. "Costs too much. Besides, Christians don't go to places like that. Sit down now, boys."

"But I want to see the animals," Ross whined, drawing out the words in an anguish of desire.

"See animals, see animals," Jimmy chanted, too young to know what the excitement was all about but caught up in it nevertheless.

"That's enough, boys. I don't want to hear another word about the circus," Logan said with a firmness that told them that the discussion had ended.

Ross sat in the straw and didn't say much on the long ride home. He was determined to see the circus. Nothing would stop him. As the wagon rolled along he schemed and plotted, licking the peppermint stick his uncle had given him at the Mercantile, and by the time they reached home, he had a plan.

As soon as Logan stopped in front of the house, Ross jumped down, ran across the yard, and burst into the house. "Mamma,

Mamma, guess what,'' he shouted. ''The animals are coming to town!''

''What is this about animals?'' she asked, studying the eager little face and wiping her hands on her apron.

''Elephants and tigers and lions—the circus, Mamma. There are pictures all over town. Mamma, can't we go to see them? We've never seen wild animals before, and they do tricks.''

''Oh, so it's a circus, is it? I know you would like to see it, but a circus really isn't a place where a Christian should go.''

''But, Mamma,'' Ross replied, throwing his arms around her knees and looking up with a desperate longing, ''What is wrong with seeing animals? That is nature, and we study nature on Sabbath.''

''A circus isn't nature study, Ross, not like taking a walk and seeing a deer. A lot of foolishness goes on there. Things a Christian should not be a part of.''

He lowered his voice then to a conspiratorial tone and said, ''I know what, Mamma. You can take Jimmy and me and we can sit in the tent and watch the circus while you sell magazines. There will be lots of people there, Mamma. You will be able to sell a whole bunch of papers.''

His mother grew thoughtful. Sitting down and pulling the child up on her lap, she replied, ''That is an idea, Rossie Boy. A good idea. I think we will just go to the circus. I've been told they always have a parade the day it starts. I see nothing wrong with going to the parade. You boys will get to see the animals, and I will sell magazines and give out tracts to the people who come to watch.''

The day of the parade her two sons stood watching the elephants clumping by, the lady standing on the white horse, and the great yellow-eyed cats snarling from their cages while Minnie moved among the crowd. Never in one day had she sold so many magazines. In a festive mood, people bought readily.

The boys came home excited about the circus, but for their mother it was another kind of euphoria—getting God's teachings for the last days out to a crowd of people. ''Let your light so shine'' had never had so much meaning.

So far she had dealt with magazines and tracts, but now she faced a greater challenge. One Sabbath shortly after the circus, two ministers from the Iowa Conference office came to the Afton church with a plea for help from the church schools in the state. Since the parishioners were for the most part unable to donate money, the men asked people to sell the book *Christ's Object Lessons* and give the proceeds to the church.

When they asked for volunteers, a few timid hands went up, among them Minnie's. The conference officials determined a quota for the Afton church, and the two men left a big box of books in the back of the church.

As Minnie and Logan rode home, the burden of selling those books rested heavily upon her. "I know I should try it," she told him, "but I am afraid."

"You afraid?" he laughed, "I don't know how many papers you have sold around the country. And that day at the circus—they went like hot cakes."

"But they were only ten cents. These big books cost a whole dollar. I don't know—"

"I think we should help with this. What say we pledge to sell a hundred books?" her husband suggested.

"One hundred books? Impossible. We'd never get that many sold and then we would be stuck with them."

"I'll help you. I do have some good contacts with the farmers around here."

Reluctantly she agreed and began to map out her campaign, but in spite of Logan's optimism about it, one hundred books loomed on the horizon like a mountain.

C H A P T E R

5

Saleslady

Minnie and the two boys set out early one day with books piled behind them in the buggy. It was a morning with high fair skies when nothing could ever go wrong. Bob-o-links, hysterical bits of feathers, exploded out of the sky, warbling as they fell to earth while meadow larks sang from fence posts. The dew was drying in the sun and it was cool yet, but it would be hot later on.

She decided to begin around the old home place where she had grown up and where her mother and father, Elias and Mary Ann Day, still lived. It was 15 miles away, and since she had not been home for some time, she and the boys planned to stay for a few days, visiting with her family and selling books in the neighborhood.

As they approached her home, Minnie felt some apprehension as she remembered the unpleasant scene at her last visit. Ever since joining the Seventh-day Adventist Church she had been eager to share her faith with her family, but they had been less than happy with her new religion. In fact, they believed that she had disgraced them. On that last visit Elias Day, her father, had shouted at her that he had not educated her to go out and join such a crazy church. "When you can't sit down to the table and eat your own mother's cooking," he had stormed, "when you turn up your nose at good pork chops and a nice warm cup of coffee, I don't know what the world is coming to."

He started to walk away, only to return to yell at her as she climbed into the buggy. "And another thing—the craziest of all—is that notion you have of going to church on Saturday. When the neighbors ask about it, I just don't know what to say."

Her own temper flared at that and she exclaimed, "You are crazy yourself if you think I have to ask the neighbors about my own personal beliefs."

Then he stalked off toward the barn, and with a forlorn good-bye from her mother, Minnie drove off. She had not seen the family since.

Today she determined that nothing would set off that kind of anger again. She vowed that she would not mention her religion. Warmed by the memories of her childhood, she and the boys entered the lane leading to the house where she had once lived. Calls from every quarter greeted them as one and then another saw them and came running. "It's Minnie and the boys," the shout went up, and soon the family escorted the travelers to the house.

Grandma Day sent Roy out to get a couple of chickens for dinner which she scalded and plucked and cut up for frying, talking as she worked. Ross and Jimmy ran out to see the new calf with cousins John and Ellie as Minnie helped her mother and caught up to date on the family news.

"It's so good to be here, Ma," she said. "Just like old times, you and me working together. Makes me feel like a little girl again. I want to hear about everyone now—how they are doing in school—their jobs—everything."

Grandma Day told her about Jossie and Blanche who were working in town and Myrtle going to teacher training school at Osceola. "She wants to be a teacher like you, Minnie. Clyde and Clarence are a big help to your pa now," she continued as she held an apple pie up and trimmed off the crust. "Big strapping fellows anyway, and you should see how Elsie and Roy work after school and in harvest. Even John and Ellie do chores—gathering eggs and such. We are right proud of our family, your pa and I."

The conversation went on about the family, the neighbors, and the farm. Mrs. Day did not mention Minnie's new religion that had caused such a furor the last time, but a small nagging thought in the back of her daughter's mind reminded her that she was here not merely to visit but to sell books and quite possibly open up the old wound. She decided to deal with it after dinner and hopefully in a tactful way.

When the meal was ready the family gathered around the table and stared appreciatively from one steaming bowl to another—white, creamy mashed potatoes with melted home-made butter running down, crisp fried chicken, gravy, corn and green beans from the garden, hot cornbread, and over on the side board they could see the pies. "This looks like Thanksgiving," Clyde exclaimed.

"It is Thanksgiving, son," Elias Day said gravely. "Your sister is here with us again—and my grandsons. Shall we bow for prayer." His prayer, long and detailed, began by thanking the Almighty in general and then getting down to particulars. John and Ellie and Jimmy fidgeted and peeped up through their fingers. Even Roy shifted in his chair and opened one eye from time to time. A sigh of relief went up around the table at the "amen."

Elias raised his head and the pious expression faded. Even his voice changed as he said heartily, "Dive in! If you go away hungry, it's your own fault. How many drumsticks do we have here, Mother?"

The conversation at the table turned to crops and weather and the new teacher—young and pretty—and of the farmer courting her, one of the Martin boys on the next farm. "The Martins is rich," Grandma Day said seriously.

"He comes courtin' in one of them new-fangled buggies, and you should see his horse—a Morgan!" Clarence added.

Grandma, her face round as a holly berry with soft little whiskers growing about her mouth, shuttled between table and stove and hovered over her guests. "Eat now," she urged.

"Ma," Minnie replied, "sit down and eat. Let me fill that bowl."

But she took the dish from her daughter, saying, "Now you are company."

The dishes had been cleared away and they were eating the pie when Elias said, "Minnie, it's been a right long time since you was here. Where you been keeping yourself?"

"You know how it is on the farm, Pa. Something all the time. First it was the chickens with the roup and then one of the horses went lame and Bessie had a calf and it got the scours, and I had a terrible time saving it."

"Scours is a bugger," Grandma agreed. "Ross, do you help take care of the calf?"

"Sure, Grandma," he answered around a mouthful of pie, adding importantly, "I even milk Bessie when Mamma goes to town to sell magazines." He returned to his pie unaware of the bombshell he had dropped. The conversation and the comfortable sounds of eating stopped and the room grew silent as all eyes focused upon his mother.

Elias's fork clattered to the table and his face turned red. "Does what?" he shouted.

"It's my missionary work, Pa," she stammered, feeling like a little girl who had done wrong. Pushing the emotions aside, she plowed on with her explanation. "I go to town every Thursday and sell magazines so I can earn money for my missionary projects. They are Christian magazines, they—I—"

No one moved for a moment and then Clyde looked at Clarence and tapped his temple with his finger. They both shook their heads and resumed eating. Roy and Elsie began to giggle, and Myrtle looked up to say with her mischievous grin, "Who'd a thought I'd have a peddler for a sister."

Troubled, Grandma Day sat looking down, folding her apron in little accordion pleats. "Can't you find another way to get money for your missionary work, Minnie?" she asked quietly.

"But, Ma, selling Christian magazines is part of my missionary work. I meet so many people who are searching for truth." She took a deep breath and looked at the stricken faces around the table before adding in a firm voice. "In fact, I plan to go out in this neighborhood while I am here and sell books to help our church schools."

At this Elias, who had been jabbing savagely at his pie, gasped, and waving his fork in the air as if it were a weapon, barked, "Not as long as you're in this house!"

"I didn't think you would care, Pa. I thought you would be glad to see the boys and me and have a nice, long visit."

"You are welcome here any time. You know that, but no daughter of mine will be a common book agent. I have no use for book agents. I won't let one in the door," and Elias brought his huge fist down on the table so hard the dishes rattled.

"Pa, listen to me. I feel it is my duty to do this. Please don't make it hard for me."

Her father pushed back from the table, his pie now untouched, and muttered as he went out to start chores, "My daughter a book agent. A disgrace, that's what it is. I will be ashamed to meet any of my neighbors—ashamed!"

The next morning Grandma was only too happy to have her grandsons for the day, but as she watched Minnie get ready to go out, her wrinkled little face was perplexed and anxious. "I don't know why you have to do this when your pa is so against it. You know how he feels about peddlers," she said, wiping her eyes on the dish towel.

With her shawl and bonnet on and her prospectus in hand, Minnie turned at the door. "I am sorry you and Pa feel this way, Ma, but it is something I have to do."

"I wish you would stay here and visit today. We haven't seen you for such a long time."

"We will have a nice visit this evening. I'm not trying to hurt you and Papa. I'm just doing what I think God wants me to do."

"Well, go on then. I just don't know which way to turn, your pa so mad and all." Quickly she stuffed a little sack of lunch in her daughter's hand.

As Minnie started toward the road she felt none of the joy she had dreamed of, only a sadness that made her feet drag and her spirits droop. Thinking about the ridicule from the neighbors her father had predicted, she shrank from the task before her. The courage she had mustered when she defended herself at the dinner table had vanished.

Once on the road she stopped at the corner and thought to return to the house, but a verse from the Bible drove her on: "He that putteth his hand to the plow and turneth back is not worthy of me." Bowing her head she prayed for strength and for success, not only in the sale of the book, but for the book itself that it might influence the homes in the neighborhood.

All that day she drove from one place to another and the old friends and neighbors were delighted with her visit and with the books she sold. When she came back that evening waving a handful of dollar bills, the family could only stand and stare. Was this their shy little Minnie?

"Did you go to the Tillman's?" someone asked.

"Oh, yes. I got there just before dinner and they insisted I eat with them. Thanks for the lunch, Ma, but I didn't need it. I even had afternoon lunch at the Roseland's. You know how those Norwegians are about lunch."

"What about the Wilsons? Did you stop there?"

"Oh, yes. They bought two books. One for their married daughter."

For the rest of that week she went out every day and had equal success. Not only that, but not one word of criticism did Elias hear from the neighbors. In fact, Minnie received praise on every side, so his fragile pride was saved.

That Friday afternoon she headed home and the next day in church gave a glowing report of sales and missionary contacts. No one else had sold a single book—even James Sype.

James found the farm kept him too busy, and, hearing of his daughter-in-law's accomplishment, said smoothly, "I'll let you use a horse and buggy if you'll sell my share. I can't seem to get out with the harvesting and all."

"You aren't alone there," she replied. "A lot of folks can't work it in. Mrs. Cary has offered to keep house for me while I sell hers, and the Johnsons will help Logan harvest corn if I take care of theirs. Looks like I have a fulltime job for a while."

"Well, do we have a deal?" her father-in-law persisted.

"It's a deal. I really don't mind going out and selling. I love it, in fact."

"How about Logan, has he sold any?"

"Not one. He was eager to order them, but can't seem to find time to sell any."

Almost single-handedly she sold enough books to enable her church to meet its quota. At campmeeting that year someone announced that only one person in the Iowa Conference had surpassed her in book sales—Elder T. H. Jeys, a minister of long standing.

CHAPTER

6

First Fruits

Winter had settled grimly over the countryside that December day when Minnie met Inga Fredricks. It was on a Sabbath, a day before snowfall when the landscape was a muted brown, and the only sound was the hushed clop-clop of the horses' hooves as the family drove to church. They passed woods and fields where the trees, dark pilgrims beneath slate skies, plodded across weary hills.

They had left early for the seven-mile drive, the children huddled under blankets against the cold. As they passed a house well off the road, Minnie pointed and said, "Logan, I believe someone has moved into the old Hagan house. We have a few minutes this morning, so I think I will go in and welcome them. See that the boys stay in the buggy so they don't get dirty before church," she cautioned as she started up to the house.

Before she knocked, the door burst open and a tall, square woman stood in the doorway. A desperate smile of welcome told of her loneliness. The old country face with high cheek bones and thin lips just missed being beautiful, and she had pulled her lovely blond hair tightly back and did it up in a knot. "Come in, come in. Let me take your coat and get you something to eat," she pleaded in a sing-song Scandinavian accent.

Minnie held up a hand in protest. "I just stopped by to get acquainted and welcome you to the neighborhood. I can only stay a minute. My husband and boys are out in the buggy."

"You can't stay then?" Disappointment clouded her blue eyes and she rushed on, "Oh, but it is nice to see another woman. I don't see nobody. My man is away working all the time, and this is not like home. I sometimes think I will die out here and no one will know."

"Well, I want you to know you have neighbors," Minnie assured her. "We are on our way to church now, but we will stop again."

"On your way to church—you are Jews then?"

"No, we are Seventh-day Adventists."

"I never heard of that in Wisconsin where we come from. I am a Lutheran. Lars, my man, is Catholic, but he don't never go. I don't get to church anymore. How I miss going to church, but the mister, he has to work all of the time, even on Sunday, and he can't take me."

Minnie tore herself away, promising to return Monday afternoon so she and Mrs. Fredricks could study the Bible together.

"Logan," she exclaimed as she climbed back into the buggy, "this lady wants me to come Monday and study the Bible with her. My first Bible study!"

"Mamma, does she have any little boys?" Ross wanted to know.

"And chee chees?" added Jimmy, who had developed a fascination for baby chicks in spite of the tragic time when he had unwittingly squeezed one to death in his enthusiasm.

"She is an older lady, Ross, so if she does have a boy, he is probably grown up and has a home of his own. Yes, Jimmy, I suppose she has chickens in the back yard, but I didn't see them."

"I won't touch them, Mamma," the boy promised seriously, putting his hands behind his back. "I'll just watch them run around."

Monday morning Minnie rushed around to finish up the washing and fix dinner. When she called the two boys in from play, she announced, "Now, boys, we're going to Mrs. Fredricks. I want you to sit quietly while I study the Bible with her. If you don't disturb us, I'll give you each a penny. Do you think you can do that?"

Both pairs of big brown eyes widened in surprise. A whole penny to spend! They couldn't believe their good fortune. As they raced to get their caps and sweaters they discussed their wealth and how they would spend it.

"We'll go to Sype's Mercantile."

"I think I'll get a pep'mint tick."

"How about some commies?"

"Or a haw breaker? They last a looong time."

Wearing her good dress, the long blond hair rolled neatly back, Mrs. Fredricks waited at the door when they arrived. She soon held Jimmy in her ample lap and showed Ross pictures of Norway in an old book. Then while the two women studied the Bible together, the boys sat quietly, remembering the penny.

"What good boys," Mrs. Fredricks said after the study. "Come out in the kitchen and let's see what we can find."

Ross and Jimmy watched while she bustled around and spread out a feast on the table. It was Norwegian food, strange and exotic: kringla, paper thin lefsa spread with butter and sugar and rolled up and when you bit into it you heard a satisfying crunch of sugar. One plate held tiny rich cookies shaped like stars which she called spritz. Besides that there were little sandwiches made with soft cheese and glasses of milk.

Minnie was a plain, no nonsense cook herself, and the sight of such food almost overwhelmed the boys who at first could only just stare from one thing to another.

"Eat now," the woman urged. "I know how hungry little boys get. I had three little boys and two girls, but they are grown up now and far away. Eat, Missus," and she pushed the plate of kringla toward Minnie.

Each Monday after that Minnie went to study with Mrs. Fredricks, accompanied by her boys who were eager to earn another penny and to see what goodies would be piled on the kitchen table with Mrs. Fredricks, huge and smiling, urging, "just one more of these little cookies." Each week she put some in a sack for Jimmy to take home to his father. The child handed them out importantly as he lisped, "These are from Mrs. Fledlicks on the other side of the lailload."

Inga Fredricks was hungry, not only for human friendship, but also for spiritual food, and she accepted all that Minnie presented. One Monday Inga's husband was there, not working because of a toothache.

"Lars, this is the lady I was telling you about," his wife said. Mr. Fredricks nodded curtly and grunted, his face unsmiling and hawklike. His cold, grey eyes fastened briefly on Minnie and then shifted away. A tall, spare man he walked with a decided limp, the result of an improperly set leg, broken while working on a fishing boat in Norway. Limping over to a corner chair in back of Minnie, he retreated behind a newspaper while the two women began the study.

Ross and Jimmy sat on the floor facing him, each playing with a toy and at first not making a sound. The two women in deep discussion about the state of the dead didn't notice the boys' suppressed giggles and whispers at first. Every once in a while there would be a slight rattle of the newspaper, and a burst of childish laughter which they tried in vain to muffle.

Their mother frowned and shushed them, and after the study she stalked out, followed by her two shame-faced little sons. At the road she demanded, "What was wrong with you boys? There will be no penny for you today. I was so humiliated." She slapped the lines over Nell's broad rump, causing the horse to break into a faster trot than usual.

"But Mamma," Ross protested, close to tears, "it was Mr. Fredrick's fault. He made funny faces behind you. He waved his hands when you waved your hands and he opened his mouth real wide. He made us laugh."

"Mr. Fledlicks was funny, Mamma," Jimmy added. "He went like this," and he pulled his eyes down with his hands and stuck out his tongue.

"We couldn't help laughing," Ross added glumly.

A few days later Minnie heard a knock at the door and on the threshold stood Mr. Fredricks, tall and awkward, hat in hand, shifting his weight from one foot to the other.

"Morning, Mrs. Sype," he said. "It ain't easy for me to eat crow, but I want to tell you I am sorry for the way I tried to disturb your study the other day. You have meant a lot to my missus, and I—I—well, I want to hear about all of them things, too." The strange light-colored eyes softened almost to tears, and when he put out a work-hardened hand, Minnie grasped it in hers.

From then on they gave studies in the evening so Mr. Fredricks could participate. Logan went too and led the singing, having discovered that Mr. Fredricks had a good, deep bass, not always on key, but with a richness that added timbre to the songfests.

By spring the Sypes had the Fredricks well prepared for baptism, and one Sabbath day the pastor held the service. As they walked down to the river the sun was warm on their backs, but the water was still cold from winter. Ducks flew over to settle down further on, but their loud quacking did not intrude.

The entire church stood on the bank of the river singing, "Just as I am without one plea—"

"My dear Sister Inga—"

"My dear Brother Lars—"

And each in turn was buried in the water and stood up, shaking off the bright drops that shone in the sun like jewels.

CHAPTER

7

To the Frontier

The Sypes felt that one could find no lovelier spot for a home than the farm in Union County, Iowa, where they lived. Situated amidst the breaks of the Grand River and its numerous creeks, it nestled in rolling hills covered with oak and hickory trees and hazelnut brush. In the spring, the deep, hollow call of the male prairie chickens resounded across the fields as they performed their elaborate mating dance. Huge maple trees surrounded the house, and fields stretched away on all sides, separated by osage orange hedges.

Minnie loved the farm and the endless variety of the changing seasons. She felt fulfillment and challenge in the simple tasks of raising chickens, milking the cows, and tending her garden. In the fall she filled the cellar shelves with jars of fruits and vegetables. She thought that nothing would ever take her away from the farm.

Logan, however, had begun to tire of the routine of farm labor and chaffed under the restraint of farming with his father. It was hard for him and the older man to work together, Logan being a dreamer and James a doer. At times the son withdrew into silence, thinking dark thoughts he shared with no one. All of this worried Minnie, who was a doer herself, not given to introspection.

On January 7, 1898, the couple had a third child, a little girl they named Anna. As she held the baby, Minnie didn't dream that she and her husband would ever do anything but till their acres and at last die here and be buried in the old cemetery behind the church. After they were gone their sons would farm it and their sons after them.

But the century was about to turn, and changes were taking place in the world beyond, and Logan felt it. While his wife worked in contentment, he knew a nagging uneasiness. It had started when Riley Kirks from the Afton church moved out to Wyoming. Letters came back from time to time destined to foster unrest in those like Logan. Kirks described another world, the frontier with its wide vistas, and to anyone dissatisfied with his present life, it loomed out there like a paradise. When Logan first read the letters he brooded on the idea, saying nothing, secretly thinking that he could endure farming in Iowa no longer but must set off for the West himself.

Kirks had gone out to Sheridan, Wyoming, the previous autumn just before snowfall to work in a mining camp. Now he returned to sell his place in Iowa. Meeting him in town at the general store, Logan heard firsthand of high adventures and money-making opportunities in the Higby mining camp.

"There are jobs galore out there," Kirks assured him. "Why, take you, now. You could get a job caring for the miners' horses, a real easy job and good wages, too. And Minnie—well, Minnie would have a job teaching school in no time. And the best part," here he drew closer and lowered his voice, "the best part is that it is a great mission field. You should see the poor souls out there just waiting for someone like you folks to bring the truth to them.

"Why on weekends them miners are plumb wore out from the week's work and are just waiting to flock to Sunday School—but they ain't none. You could start out by having Sunday School and after a while, of course, you can bring them around to the Sabbath." He ended by saying, "Why don't you pull up stakes and come on out West, the land of opportunity?"

Logan carefully planned how he should bring the topic of the West—the land of opportunity according to Riley Kirks—up to his wife. He himself was convinced that he should go, but he knew how she loved Iowa and the farm. That evening after supper he began casually, "I ran into Brother Kirks down at the store today."

"Riley Kirks? I thought he was out West someplace."

"He was, he is, but he is back for a few days—some business about his place. In fact he's selling it. Uh, he was telling me about good jobs out there where he is in Wyoming." Getting up from his chair, he began to pace nervously about the room.

Minnie stared down at her mending, a warning sounding in her mind like the ringing of a little bell.

Her husband plunged on with the details of his conversation with

Riley Kirks, and she remained silent until he said, "We ought to look into those good jobs out there and that missionary work. I think we should move out to Wyoming."

Stunned, all she could manage to get out was a cry of outrage. "Move to Wyoming! Logan Sype, are you out of your mind? If you think I am going to drag my children to some wild place out west, you have another think coming!"

"But what about me?" he wailed. "You know what the farm dust does to my asthma."

"What do you think mine dust will do to it? You wouldn't last a week in those mines. The whole plan is ridiculous."

"But Riley says there are other good jobs. I wouldn't have to labor in the mines."

"I don't care what Riley says. He always did have an itchy foot and a fine way of talking, but that is all it is—just talk."

"But Minnie, this is a chance for me to prove myself—to do something on my own."

"I won't even talk about leaving this nice farm where we have security and your father is close to help us out."

"That's just the trouble!" he shouted, banging his fist on the table in an unusual burst of temper. "I am tired of being my father's hired man. I want to do something on my own for a change."

"But you are on your own. You are running this farm all by yourself."

"I am not really making the big decisions, and you know it. I am constantly under my father's shadow. I need to branch out, to be independent. The truth is, my father is smothering me." With that he slammed out of the house, banging the door behind him.

Minnie sat quietly for a long time, thinking about the community of Sand Creek Township: the peacefulness and the ancient, stable values there in the people, typical old American stock, sturdy, God-fearing folk. The friendships formed here went back beyond childhood, back generations, bringing to the relationships a comforting continuity that gave life in such neighborhoods a deep meaning. She sighed and got up, slow and stiff, and began to prepare dinner.

Again and again Logan brought the subject up. *He is like a dog with a bone,* she thought, *worrying it, gnawing at it, burying it, only to dig it up and begin to chew on it again.* Her husband spoke at great lengths about the evangelism they could do out West, but Minnie was adamant. She had all the witnessing opportunities that she could do right there. At length she said, "This is a wild, impractical scheme, and besides, your father won't hear of it."

"Ah, but he will hear of it. He agrees that it might be a good move for all of us," Logan announced triumphantly.

When Minnie talked with James she found it was true, for he also had tried to reason with his son but found him obsessed by the idea. "So maybe it is best to let him go, try his wings, get this restlessness out of his system," he concluded.

Finally she agreed to move and sadly began to pack, a task she had to do alone, for Logan, like a bird released from a cage, departed immediately for Wyoming to find a place to live and to get one of those jobs just waiting out there in the west. Sitting alone in the bare house with boxes piled around her, Minnie waited for the men with wagons to take her and the children and everything they owned to the railway station.

Once on the train she held Anna in her arms and stared bleakly out of the window at the changing terrain. She sat slumped in dejection while the train roared and clacked and whistled and slid to a stop and jerked forward again. Feeling helpless and alone, she took out her Bible and read for a while.

When she paused to meditate, it seemed as if the clickity-clack of the wheels on the track seemed to be saying, "Don't want to go, don't want to go." Then she prayed, "Lord, You know how I feel about this move. Give me courage, Lord, and may Thy name be glorified wherever You lead me."

She slept then and when she awoke the wheels seemed to sing, "With God I will, with God I will."

Logan met them at the station in Sheridan with a team and wagon to take them to the Higby mining camp where he now worked, six miles down a rutted trail. As he drove he talked excitedly, not pausing to notice how quiet Minnie had grown, weary from the journey and disheartened by the raw, cheerless town of Sheridan and the forbidding face of the countryside.

When they started out golden trees rustled beneath fair skies, but before they had gotten far out of town clouds rolled in, the sky lowered, and the wind bore down from the Northwest. Small, snowflakes hurled out of the sullen sky and spit and hissed along the frozen ruts. Minnie and the children shivered in their thin coats.

Mountains brooded in the distance and on every side the wild, bitter landscape fell away, cold, unfriendly and foreboding. The camp itself was nothing but a shabby collection of shacks scattered about in a gully. The settlement seemed to center around a big barn-like building with the word SALOON printed above the door.

Loud laughter and shouts burst from it, and as they drove past, a man staggered out, grinning foolishly at the sight of the travelers. He drew himself to attention and bowed, sweeping the dust with his hat. "Oh, a lady," he slurred, "welcome to Higby."

Logan drove around behind the saloon and pulled up to a grey miner's shanty not much bigger than the chicken house back on the farm. Minnie stared for a long time at the tottering little shack perched on the edge of nowhere with its rickety porch that leaned on two shaky poles for support. The door sagged on rusty hinges and protested loudly when her husband pushed it open.

The inside was as bad as the outside—dark, cheerless, and cold. Logan stirred up the fire in the cook stove and pushed a pot of stew to the front to warm up. "Well, this is home—for a while anyway. We'll get something better later. But for now, kind of fun, hey boys? Sorta like camping out." Their father rambled on, trying to straighten things up, hardly daring to look at his wife.

So this is home, she thought, longing for the cozy farmhouse she had left behind.

CHAPTER

8

In the Mining Camp

In spite of Riley Kirk's fine rhetoric about evangelism on the frontier, Minnie did not notice anyone longing to go to church on Sunday. All she saw in the bleak, barren, mining camp were men and women, beaten and defeated by life, who spent their evenings and weekends in the saloon. As for Riley Kirks himself, he had already gone, having followed another will-o'-the-wisp to California.

Strangers were no novelty at the Higby mining camp where new faces appeared daily with wanderers stopping briefly and then going on. The community largely ignored the Sypes at first, the way people do toward newcomers out of some vague fear or suspicion, but the children came over at once to play with the boys or just to stand and stare as if they had nothing else to do, nowhere else to go.

Minnie watched them as they played in the road and between the houses or clustered on her doorstep like flies. Clad in cast-off clothing, many with no shoes, they had tangled, unkempt hair and runny noses. But it was their eyes that moved her the most. Not the round, questioning eyes of farm children, but rat's eyes that slid away uneasily and clouded with terror at a sudden move. She longed to gather them up and turn them loose in an Iowa apple orchard in the fall when the apples were ripe.

Since she obviously could not witness to the grown-ups at first, she knew she must start with the children. She organized a little Sabbath School, and as many as 35 children came on Sabbath to listen to stories and sing.

After she had been there long enough so she knew the regulars from the transients, Minnie began going out to visit the women. Putting Anna in her buggy she went from home to home, leaving tracts and speaking kindly to the wives of the miners, many of them as hollow-eyed and wretched as the children.

When she stood at the door of the shanty where Matilda Swenson lived with her husband, Swen, and their big brood of red-haired children, she hesitated. From within came the sounds of loud talk and laughter and the clink of glasses, but committed to calling on everyone, she knocked anyway. Matilda herself threw open the door. A big, unkempt woman, red hair sprouting from her head like corkscrews, she threw her arms around Minnie and pulled her into the room. "Why, Mrs. Sype, come in and join us."

Several women sat around a cluttered table drinking beer. Raising their glasses, they beckoned Minnie to join them. Nell Kelly, a tough, tight-lipped little woman noted for her alcoholic consumption, stood up with a foaming mug in her hand and slurred, "Here, a nice glass of beer on a hot day. Good for you."

"No, thank you," Minnie replied. "I never drink beer, never have. I just stopped to leave you something interesting to read."

Mrs. Kelly took a long drink, wiped her mouth with the back of her hand, and turning to the others, said in her thin, slightly tipsy voice, "Poor Mrs. Sype is not free to drink what she chooses."

"Don't pity me. I am happy without the beer."

Hiccuping and leaning toward her, Mrs. Kelly shook her head gravely and said, "Poor Mrs. Sype can't have any beer and doesn't have any fun. No beer, no fun, poor woman. You are not free."

"The truth is, I am the happiest woman in this camp. I don't have to spend money for beer, money that is needed for food and clothing. I am the free woman. You are the slave."

They stared at her a moment, then Matilda put her arm around her shoulders. "Mrs. Sype, I believe you are the free woman."

Minnie visited the home frequently, and one day Matilda said longingly, "Oh, Mrs. Sype, I wish I knew how to pray."

"Did you never pray?"

"No, I never heard anyone pray in my home. My mother never prayed, and I long for something more than this life. I wish I was a good Christian. Will you teach me to pray?" The broad, freckled face was sad, the eyes yearning.

"I'll be happy to teach you. It is impossible for us to live as Christians in this world without prayer. Our Saviour found it necessary to pray and we must pray.''

After Minnie read from the Bible and offered prayer, she said, ''All right, Matilda, you pray now.''

''Really, Mrs. Sype, I can't pray. I don't know what to say.''

''Will you say the words after me then?''

So Minnie prayed and Matilda repeated the words after her.

Logan didn't get the job taking care of the miners' horses that Riley Kirks had promised, but had to work in the mines. He found the mine dust more irritating than the hay dust had been, and his lung condition worsened. But still he sweetened the atmosphere of the mining camp by singing as he walked to work.

Ed Severson, a miner from Minnesota, stopped him one morning and said, ''That is some fine singing.'' A wistful look crossed his dust-grimed face. ''You know, we used to get together for singing back home. We should do that here. Give us something to do evenings besides go to the saloon.''

After Logan organized a singing school, each Thursday night the camp's rough men and women joined in gospel songs. It even made a little change in the camp, for often instead of cursing or bawdy songs, many of the men sang hymns as they walked to and from work.

After a few months in the mines, Logan realized he could not stand up under such heavy, dusty work. Asthma had plagued him since childhood, and now the mine dust triggered a bad attack. As he sat gasping for breath one day, he wheezed, ''What am I going to do? I can't take this any longer.''

''Why don't you ask Mr. Hayes if he has something else you can do?'' his wife suggested.

''I did. I asked him today and he said that the man who took care of the horses and mules was quitting at the end of the week. I can have his job, but—''

''There you go,'' she interrupted, ''the Lord opened up a way to get you out of that dirty mine and you hesitate.''

''Well, He better open up a way to change Mr. Hayes' mind then because he said if I take the job I'll have to work Saturdays. There is no way out. I am going to have to go back down in that mine even—'' and a great hacking cough tore through his chest.

''Oh, no, you won't, Logan Sype. I'm going right over and have a talk with Mr. Hayes,'' and she bustled out the door before Logan could stop her.

The camp superintendent was in his office perched on a high stool working on a ledger. Hat on head as usual, he waved his cigar at her and called out, "Howdy, Mrs. Sype. Have a chair. What can I do for you?"

Ignoring the only chair in the stuffy little room, Minnie stood with arms folded and said, "Mr. Hayes, I'll come right to the point. It's about my husband. He isn't able to manage the heavy mine work because of his health, having always had weak lungs. Don't you have something he can do that is not so strenuous?"

"Yes, Mrs. Sype, I told him only this morning that he can have charge of the horses and mules. Of course, he will have to work Saturdays same as any other day. I can't keep him on otherwise."

"Never, Mr. Hayes. He will never work on Saturday. If you let him go because he doesn't do his work or because he steals or something like that, I could understand, but if you fire him for Sabbath-keeping, we will be glad to leave this camp, even if we have to go out afoot."

"Remember, Mrs. Sype, you have children to support."

"Yes, and we will do all we can to support them, but we will never break one of God's commandments to do so," she declared firmly as she turned to leave, and with her hand on the doorknob shot back at him, "Some people steal horses to support their families. That is no worse than stealing God's time."

He slipped down from his stool and frowned intently at his now unlit cigar before saying wearily, "All right, all right. I know when I'm licked. Tell your husband to report at the corral tomorrow morning."

That winter an epidemic of measles broke out in the camp, leaving sick children in almost every house lying miserably on the floor wrapped in thin blankets. Ross and Jimmy came down with it, and when they were still covered with the measles the coal supply ran out, and the company failed to deliver any for several days. In the meantime, Minnie had to keep the children warm, for the shack was as cold as the out-of-doors, so she told them to stay in bed and tried to make them cover up.

The boys were still sick enough to lie still, but Anna, who was just getting the disease, tumbled about and laughed and cried and caught cold, causing the measles to "settle in her throat" as Minnie explained it. The child grew extremely ill and someone had to hold her upright to prevent her from choking. Day after day Anna fought for breath, turning red as she coughed and then blue as she gasped for air until it seemed as if she would die.

Cradling the little girl in her arms, Minnie thought about how she missed her evangelistic visits. If I can't go to them, she decided, they must come to me. So she invited the women to visit her home one day a week to quilt.

Any get-together at the Higby mining camp was a party, so the women brought cookies and lemonade as well as sewing materials. Only three showed up for the first meeting, but gradually more and more joined the group. As they sewed, Minnie read to them, her baby's head resting on her shoulder. Not only was it a time for good fellowship, but Minnie shared her faith.

With the proceeds from the quilts they sold, they bought *The Little Friend*, and *Youth's Instructor* for the children. Some of the money also went to help the poor and needy among them.

Even hard-bitten Goldie McBride joined the quilters and one day confided to Minnie, "You know, Mrs. Sype, my life seemed hopeless when I started coming to your sewing circle. I felt I couldn't handle a drinking husband and five squabbling children any longer. Then I came to your home and saw how patient you were. How you held that sick baby and didn't complain. Then I went back home and tried to be more kind and patient with my family."

All of the women were concerned about Anna. After the child had coughed herself into exhaustion and lay limp in Minnie's arms, Tillie, a seasoned mother of seven, said, "Mrs Sype, a little bit of whiskey would do that baby a world of good—loosens up the phlegm."

"That's right," another mother chimed in as she looked up over her sewing. "There's nothing like a drop of whiskey to snap a person out of a sick spell."

The others all nodded, but Minnie hugged the frail little form to herself and said testily, "Not one drop of whiskey will go down my child's throat. God won't let her die for want of a little whiskey."

By using hydrotherapy treatments she had learned in Iowa, Minnie brought her daughter through her illness. Anna regained her health, much to the surprise of the neighbors who predicted she would be buried in the dainty dress her Aunt Myrtle had sent for the child's first birthday.

After that the women summoned Minnie when a child in camp took sick, and they referred to her as "doctor." An epidemic of cholera infantum broke out and they called for her any hour of the day or night to tend sick children.

The miners were grateful for what the Sypes had done for them and even Mrs. Hayes, the wife of the superintendent, commented, "It's funny what a difference two people can make. Things have changed since you came and started to work with these folks."

Logan had no more trouble about Sabbath observance and a job opened up for Minnie when the nearby school asked her to teach the spring term. One big problem at the mining camp did bother the couple.

Their two boys were changing in subtle ways. There began to appear a roughness in their speech, a little carelessness in their habits, and it all pointed to a trend their parents didn't like and, in fact, feared. It worried them to think of the boys approaching manhood in such surroundings. The children they played with and went to school with were uncouth and irreverent, and it was beginning to rub off.

"What can we do?" Minnie and Logan asked one another. And then a letter arrived from James Sype. "Can you come back to Iowa to help me on the farm?" he wrote. "I don't seem to have the energy I used to have, and it is hard to find good help. I need you, Logan, and we miss Minnie and the children. Please consider returning."

Logan studied the letter and then his eyes strayed around the cramped, shabby little shanty they called home. He never had found Minnie that better house that he'd promised. "You want to go back, don't you?" he said to her.

"You know I do."

"Things haven't quite worked out here, have they? And we must think of the boys. Even though we do have a few of these miners attending Sabbath School with us, our first concern has to be our children."

He walked over to the rough shelf he had built and took the books down, stacking them in a box. "It hasn't exactly been like Riley Kirks promised, has it? Well, Minnie, let's start packing."

CHAPTER

9

The Nickols Place

The train hurried on ever eastward, screaming into the darkness, carrying the family out of Wyoming, across the flatness of Nebraska, and into Iowa. When low rolling hills appeared, Minnie knew she was close to home and an inner joy welled up. Logan, however, slumped down in his seat, eyes on the floor, not speaking.

"Won't it be just grand to get home again?" she gushed. "Back to the farm in Iowa. I can hardly wait!" She pressed her face to the window and then glanced over at her husband who was in one of his moods. "What's the matter, Logan? You look sick."

He gazed straight ahead for a long time before he turned to her, his dark, hopeless eyes staring out of his thin face. "In a way I am sick. I am sick of having to run back home to my father all of the time, of never being able to make a go of anything." The words came out in a rush, and he put his head in his hands and sighed helplessly. Helplessness was one thing Minnie could never understand. She felt a frustrated anger toward him.

"Don't talk rot. You can do anything you set your mind to. Come now. This is a new beginning. Sit up and look around." When he did not respond, she fixed her attention on the scene outside.

"Oh, look!" she exclaimed. "There's a town, a little Iowa town." She caught a glimpse of tall white houses and a church steeple and the wind flailing the giant elms that lined the street.

While she gazed at scenes that told her she was home again, Logan continued to sit in silence, alone with his dark thoughts. Her words, "You can do anything you want to," went through his head.

Maybe she could, but he perceived himself as weak and vacillating, nothing like James Sype, nor his grandfather before him, nor like Chief John Logan. *Nothing seems to work for me,* he thought. *I want to take charge of things, but it always ends up by things taking charge of me. Now if I were Chief John Logan*—and he envisioned that warrior with his enemy scalps hanging from his tribal belt.

The train ground to a halt at Afton, cutting short his dream, and all he saw was a forlorn depot in Iowa on a blustery autumn day, and he was Logan Sype being dragged back to work for his father. The children jumped down and ran like calves before a storm. Minnie was as happy as they, but her husband shuffled slowly down the steps, bent over like an old man, his face stiff with some repressed rage. His tribal belt had no trophies.

James Sype, affable and self-assured, took them out to the farm in his big two-seated surrey. They would live with Logan's parents until spring when James planned to buy them a farm. That winter Logan helped his father as he had done since boyhood. Minnie worked around the house, feeling much at home there, and again many nights that winter she studied the Bible with her father-in-law around the kitchen table.

On a day in February when they were all eating dinner, James looked up with a gleam in his shrewd eyes and said, "I've got a surprise for you." Everyone watched him as he reached for a piece of bread, buttered it, and took a bite.

"What is it, Grandpa? Tell us," Ross begged.

"Is it a new calf?" Jimmy asked.

"No, it is better than a calf."

"Are you going to take us to the circus?" Ross questioned.

"No, 'fraid not."

"Did the speckled hen hatch out some baby chickies?" Anna interjected.

"None of you are even close. I am going to have to tell you. I've bought a farm for you!"

"Is it far from here?"

"When can we see it?"

The questions came from all sides, from Minnie and the children and even Grandma Sype. Logan, however, nervously stirred his potatoes and gravy. His face tense and drawn, he did not look up as his father beamed and announced grandly, "It's the old Nickols place. You know where it is—about a mile up the road from here toward town."

"The old Nickols place?" Minnie exclaimed. "I have always loved that place! It is so home-like. Every time we pass it on our way to town I notice it. Remember, Logan, how I used to say how cozy it looked? Oh, Father, when can we go and see it?"

"As soon as we finish dinner we'll drive over to see your farm," the older man promised.

After dinner they all trooped out, James and Minnie with heads together in terse, eager discussion about the farm. The children talked of the coasting hills and the pond, but Logan hung back and paused beside his mother who was clearing the table.

"Mother," he said, "why does Father do these things—buying a farm and everything? He knows it will only make me indebted to him."

His mother, a simple and down-to-earth woman not given to expressing herself or showing affection, put her hand on his arm, giving it a gentle squeeze. "He don't mean no harm, Logan. He only wants what is best for you. Think of Minnie and the children."

"I do, Mother. I think of them all the time, but still you must know how I feel about it—" The words trailed off and he turned to follow the others.

James and the children rode in the front seat talking and pointing while Logan and Minnie sat behind. "Logan," she whispered, "if you don't want the farm, we don't have to take it. We can go someplace else. You don't have to farm."

"Where would we go? What else can I do?" and he stared bleakly at the sparkling February day, the sun on the snow and the team splashing through the softening ruts in the road. "No, this is best. Father is right," he sighed, refusing to be cheered by the false spring day when chickadees piped their spring song, "Pee wee, pee wee."

The house sat on a hill, and when Minnie walked in the door, it was as if she were returning to some dear place she had previously left. Below the hill lay a pond covered now with ice and surrounded by tattered reeds but promising ducks and red-winged blackbirds come spring. Behind the house a small apple orchard flourished, and the barn rested snug against the hills. Pastures and fields rolled away from the house, and beyond the farm itself, like a backdrop, little hills folded one upon another, covered with hickory, walnut, and oak.

The farm was small, only 70 acres, but the land was fertile and productive and it was all that Minnie had ever wanted. When they moved in a month later, as she and Logan stood looking toward those hills, she declared, "I am going to live here until the Lord comes."

The first bluebirds shivered in the gray trees, bringing on their backs the blue from some distant skies, and spring arrived in a rush of windswept days. Clouds of rising and falling blackbirds filled the bare trees like dark fruit. Logan put the crops in, working doggedly on in spite of his asthma. The days rolled on one after another like river pebbles, round and smooth, dropping into a leather bag.

When he wanted to pray, Logan found a retreat in the barn in an empty box stall where he prayed for his family, holding up each by name. The humble place with its scent of hay and oiled harnesses hanging on the wall had a feel of the sacred about it. Peace came to him in this rude structure of rough boards with motes dancing in the shafts of sunlight.

Minnie went out to the orchard when she wanted to be alone with her thoughts and with God. She often knelt there to thank God for all of His blessings and to ask for strength to carry on for Him.

In Iowa, the wind takes on a deep hollow tone late in August, sighing across the land. On this day it set the orchard trees to dancing and blew over Minnie, a yearning murmur, as she knelt in prayer. "God, all we are, all we have are Yours."

An impression came then so strong she knew it was from God. A voice whispered, "And would you sell?"

Jumping to her feet, she exclaimed, "Sell this little home? Move again? Go away I know not where?—Oh, Lord, surely this will not be."

Once again the impression came, even stronger. "And would you sell?"

Stricken for having told the Lord that all they were and all they had were His, she dared not refuse. "Yes, Lord," she murmured, "we would sell."

In her heart she hoped that it would never happen, and yet after that, in her waking or sleeping hours, she had a vague feeling of unrest, some nagging doubt. When she went out to the garden to gather vegetables, the feeling was with her, and when she carried them into the kitchen, it persisted. It was on her shoulder when she fed the chickens and gathered the eggs. Even while she prayed it was there. It never left her.

C H A P T E R

10

The Test

In spite of the vague uneasiness that hung over her, the days on the Nickols place marched in dream-like progression. The children happily played in the woods and fields and she contentedly kept house and did her farm chores. When she went out to milk the cows and they turned slowly toward her, eyes big and unsurprised, she knew some deep primal tie with them and with the earth itself, with this place.

Logan, however, moved from one grim, joyless day to another. In spite of the fact that the farm was doing well and they planned to build a new house in the fall, he wished constantly for other places, other tasks. Dogged by nebulous dreams, he took no pleasure in his work as the year turned from winter to spring and the good clean scent of the earth rose as the plow turned the furrows. Neither was there any satisfaction at harvest when he beat the wheat out of the husk and tore the ears of corn from the stalk.

He saw himself growing old and toothless, face lined and body bent over before his time until he resembled the photographs that hung in the sitting room. Those pictures of his grandfather and great-grandfather had been made when they were only 50 years old. The gaunt, forbidding faces haunted him.

When Minnie tried to talk with him she encountered only silence, and when she told him to "snap out of it" in her direct way, he only withdrew further. He perceived his return to the farm as failure on his part, and now as always, he was not doing what he desired to do but what his father wanted.

On Sabbaths after hitching the horse to the buggy for Minnie and the children, he walked the five miles to church. Because of his fine voice the congregation requested him to conduct the song service, and at home he continued to lead family worship, but still he remained a man alone.

The day the letter came he had gone to town lethargic as usual, but when he arrived home he was a changed man. Breathless he rushed into the house waving an envelope in the air. "Good news, Minnie," he shouted. "I went to the post office and there was a letter from Leo Van Wyngarden."

"Leo Van Wyngarden," she repeated in puzzlement.

"Yes, you know, Leo and Tessie Van Wyngarden, those folks from Union County who moved to the Oklahoma Territory to homestead. Here, you have to read it for yourself," and he thrust the envelope into her hands.

The long letter began with a glittering account of the opportunities in that country, which just eleven years ago had been an Indian reservation, but now was opening up for homesteading. In some detail he described the Oklahoma Land Rush, when at noon on April 22, 1889, hordes of people had raced off in wagons or buggies, on horseback, or on foot to stake out a claim.

Mr. Van Wyngarden went on to explain that he and his family had a homestead just a few miles from Indian Territory, and then the letter became more confidential as he described a homestead that was for sale. "This beautiful farm of 160 acres can be bought for only $1000. That is like stealing it. The entire farm has been fenced, the ground cultivated, and some crops planted. There is a comfortable sod house ready for a family to move into. The only reason such a farm is for sale at this price is because the man who homesteaded it took sick and had to go back to Missouri. He feels terrible about leaving, but what can he do?

"It is only ten miles from our place, and I would like to see you get this bargain, Logan, but you will have to act fast. Men are already looking at it."

Logan leaned forward tensely as his wife finished reading. Without a word she folded it, put it back into the envelope, and handed it to him.

"What do you think, Minnie? This is just what we have been looking for—160 acres, ours for the taking. Like Leo says, it's a steal. It's almost too good to be true. I say we write and tell him we'll take it. What do you say?''

''No, Logan,'' she said evenly, standing with arms folded, unmoved. ''Absolutely not. It is out of the question. I am not moving off to some uncivilized place again and that is final.''

''Uncivilized?'' he repeated with a scornful laugh. ''What do you mean? They are farmers, people like the Van Wyngardens and like us.''

''You know very well what I mean. There are wild Indians all around. Our neighbors, the Van Wyngardens, would be ten miles away. I will not drag my children to a place like that again, and you can just forget it.''

She stamped from the room and fled to her garden, but Logan followed, waving the letter like a flag of truce. ''But, Minnie, we'll have more than twice as much land as we have here. With the money we get for this place we can build a much bigger house than the one we plan to construct here. We will need more acreage when the boys are older, and this is our big chance to get more land for less money.''

''I don't want to hear any more about such nonsense.''

''Nonsense? You are calling a great opportunity like this nonsense? You and Father never give me a chance to be independent. How do you think I feel living here like a hired hand?''

''Now look here, Logan Sype. I am tired of moving all around the country. You never think about the rest of us, always yourself.'' She fought desperately to control her trembling voice. ''I am not going off on any of your wild goose chases again. If you want to go, you can, but I am staying right here.''

Folding the letter and slipping it into his pocket, her husband stumbled down the path while Minnie attacked the weeds in the garden. After a while she paused in her work to look around at the farm. It was a day in summer when the magnificent swell of the growing fields reached to the horizon. To her it was a paradise on earth, and Logan wanted to throw it all aside and reach out for some unknown frontier. She remembered Wyoming and shuddered.

Anger festered and grew on both sides, and the house grew silent and tense with it. Even the children crept about, unnaturally quiet, scattering to the fields where they ran and played.

One morning a few days later Minnie awoke early when the sun was still below the horizon. Through the window she saw a red glow promising a fine day. A single robin shattered the pre-dawn silence, its song ringing out in the still air. After other birds had taken up the chorus, she could still hear the shrill refrain of the robin echoing in the background.

Dressing quietly, she headed for the orchard. Out under the trees she prayed, "Lord, help me to know Thy will." Then she remembered that other morning in the orchard when she had heard the Lord speaking to her.

And would you sell?

Fear had seized her then. Now panic tightened her throat and squeezed her chest. "No, Lord, surely You aren't asking me to do something so senseless."

The question persisted. *Would you sell for Me?*

Head down, Minnie paced back and forth. Tears burned her eyes, a headache pounded in her temples. She leaned her cheek against the rough bark of a pear tree while her hands caressed the growing fruit. Walking, pacing, weeping, she finally drew comfort from the trees and God. Did she speak the words aloud? Later, she could not recall. "All right, Lord. You died on the cross for me, so I can give up my lovely home for You. But, Lord, if this is what You want us to do, like Gideon, I need a sign.

"I will be willing to go to Oklahoma if Logan can sell this farm for more than was paid for it and if he can get cash for it, cash right now. And if Father Sype will give his consent to our moving."

She knew that she had driven a hard bargain. The conditions seemed impossible, especially since she knew the Sypes wanted their only son close to home. As for selling the farm, who would buy a little farm in such times? A great burden rolled from her shoulders as she walked to the house and began preparing breakfast.

Logan himself had been doing some heart-searching. He wanted to break the heavy silence that hung over the household, but didn't know how. Somehow he had to reconcile his desire for happiness for his family with his yearning for independence. "I am 44 years old, and if I am ever going to make a break, it has to be now," he reminded himself grimly.

That morning he walked into the sitting room with a heavy heart. His wife and children had already gathered for worship. Listlessly he reached for the Bible, turned at random to Psalm 37, and began to read, "Trust in the Lord and do good; so shalt thou be fed. Delight thyself also in the Lord; and He shall give thee the desires of thine heart."

As he closed the Bible the anger seemed to drain from him and he said, "Mamma, I'm sorry for the way I talked to you. I guess we have been running ahead of God again. Let's leave this matter in His hands."

Tears came to her eyes and she replied, "I'm sorry, too. I hate these angry feelings and words. Why, these poor children don't know what is going to happen next." She told him of her own prayer in the orchard earlier that morning and concluded, "So we will know the Lord is leading if the place sells for more than was paid for it and if your father gives his consent to our moving."

They hugged each other and the children crowded in for a hug, too. The boys, faces bright and eager once more, talked in high, excited voices, and Anna took her doll and sang a lullaby. One evening about two weeks later when Logan sat out on the porch in the cool of the evening after a day in the fields, Bert Higgins climbed stiffly down from his buggy and walked up to the house. Their neighbor seldom, if ever, came over just to visit, and Logan wondered what brought him here as they discussed crops and weather, the way farmers everywhere talk when they meet.

Bert twisted uneasily in his chair and gazed out across the hayfield before saying, "Well, Logan, I'm going to come right out with it. I'd like to buy your farm. I've already bought the 80 acres on the other side of my place and I want to finish out my quarter section."

Logan named his price, a figure much higher than his father had paid for it, and added quickly, "I won't sell, though, unless I get cash money."

Higgins studied the hayfield once more and then drawled, "Sounds like a fair price to me, and cash won't be any problem at all. Tell you what, let's go to Afton in the morning and close the deal."

"I'll have to talk it over with my father first. Then I'll get back to you."

"All right. Just holler when you're ready."

When Logan told Minnie about the offer she could hardly believe it and stared about her kitchen in dismay as if it were going to be snatched away from her in a second. But her fears quieted when she remembered that the ultimate test yet waited. There was no way Father Sype would give his consent, and she went to bed that night untroubled and dreamed of walking peacefully in the sunlit fields with the children.

CHAPTER 11

Off to Oklahoma

Minnie was kneading bread when Logan returned from his father, the smell of the dough filling the kitchen. "Well, what did your father say?" she asked cheerfully, so sure of his response that she didn't even pause in the rhythm of her work.

"He said to accept the offer."

Unprepared for such a response, she pulled her hands from the dough and absent-mindedly peeled the sticky bits off as Logan rattled on. "He told me to get down to the bank before Higgins changes his mind. 'You'll never get a better offer,' he said."

"What about—about our moving to Oklahoma? What did he say about that?" Her voice sounded far away, forlorn.

"He thinks it may be a wise move. Nice big farm like that for a song, you might say. What with the boys growing up and all—" His voice trailed off as he saw her face and the way she continued to pluck aimlessly at the fragments of dough on her hands. In the silence that wedged between them the only sound was the clock ticking with irritating cheerfulness.

Remembering her bargain with God, Minnie spoke first. "All right," she said with a deep resigned sigh, "it looks like God is leading us to Oklahoma. Go ahead and close the sale."

Logan wasted no time in sending money for the down payment on the 160 acres of land in Oklahoma and in making plans to move. When he mentioned the sod house Leo Van Wyngarden had described as "comfortable," she held up her hands and shook her head. "I've heard enough about those sod houses to know I don't want to live in one."

They reached a compromise, deciding that he should go on ahead of the family and build a house. Knowing he would need help he persuaded her father, Elias Day, to accompany him. Anything new and different was a source of energy to Logan, and he rushed around, scarcely stopping to rest as he packed up farm tools and household goods, got the livestock ready, and chartered a railroad boxcar for the move. He and his father-in-law boarded the freight train buoyed by the mystic of going west that has lured men for countless ages.

Remaining behind to clean up the empty house, Minnie felt as if she were sweeping up her own broken dreams. Starting upstairs and finishing with the front steps, she worked on, not even pausing to cry. Finished, she set the broom in a corner of the kitchen because everyone said it was bad luck to take an old broom to a new house. She closed the door carefully, going back once more to make sure the latch caught, then drove off with a horse and buggy that James had loaned to her.

At the corner she stopped and looked back at the little farm with all of its lost hopes and dreams—and the tears came. "Don't cry," Ross said. "Mamma, Pa and Grandpa are building us a new house." But the tears only fell the faster.

Camp meeting convened in Des Moines that year and she planned to take the train west from there. While at camp meeting Walter L. Manful, a publishing leader for the Iowa Conference, asked her if she would take his son Lewis to Oklahoma with her. His wife had died recently and since he planned on moving out there in the near future, he wanted Minnie to keep the boy with her until he arrived. So she left Des Moines bound for El Reno, Oklahoma, with four children instead of three.

Before she had departed she had counted her money and calculated how much she would need for the trip. She took just enough to get them through to Weatherford, Oklahoma, where her father would meet her at the station. However, along the way the train was delayed and sat idly on a siding for several days, and she watched her carefully budgeted funds slip away.

The first day of the delay Jimmy came limping up with only one shoe, and when she learned that he had thrown the other one out of the moving train at a jackrabbit, she was furious. She spanked him soundly and then had to trudge down to the tiny town and buy him a new pair, paying more than they were worth. The children were always hungry as the days wore on and by the time the train started up her pocketbook was nearly empty.

It was a sad procession that got off the train at El Reno: a short, weary woman lugging a suitcase and a sack heavy with magazines, and four children each dragging a bag along. Minnie counted her money again and had to face the hard fact that she did not have enough to buy the tickets to Weatherford.

Once inside the depot they dropped the luggage and plopped down on the grimy bench that stretched along the wall. They stared out through the dirty window at the prairie broadening to the horizon. Separated by iron bars, a small room for the ticket agent filled one corner. Empty now and disheveled with a litter of rumpled and scattered papers on desk and floor, it had an abandoned cast. Backed into a corner stood a defiant pot-bellied stove and beside it, cold and unfriendly, an empty coal bucket. A few charred papers in the grate told of futile efforts at starting a fire.

A fine kettle of fish this is, Minnie thought to herself. *Here we are—a lone woman and four hungry children, no money, and no place to spend the night.* Once again she counted her funds. She did not have enough to purchase the tickets on to Weatherford and certainly not enough for a hotel room and supper.

"I'm hungry," Jimmy whined and then Anna began to cry, the long, shuddering, helpless sobs of an exhausted child. Ross and Lewis, gazing idly about the room, saw the "Wanted" posters that lined the walls, some new and some yellowed, frayed, and fly-specked. "Look at this one—$200 reward. He looks mean, though."

"How about this—$500 reward for information leading to the arrest of Rattlesnake Richard."

"Oh, look here, 'Wanted for murder. $1000 reward—' "

"Mamma," Ross shouted, "if we need money, look at this. All we have to do is—"

"Stop that foolishness," she commanded. "Come over here, children. We have to pray." They all bowed their heads and Minnie prayed, thanking the Lord for His goodness and mercy. "Protect us from evil," she entreated and all four pairs of little eyes strayed up to the gallery of evil faces staring down at them. She concluded by saying, "You know, Lord, we don't have any money. We need a place to stay tonight and something to eat, and we need tickets to Weatherford."

For a moment she sat with eyes closed, and taking advantage of it, Ross and Lewis sidled over to the door, but she called them back sharply. "You boys stay right here and watch these children. I've got to go out and get some money so we can buy food and get a room for tonight."

"But, Mamma," Ross protested, "where can you get money? We don't know anybody here in this town."

"Don't you worry, sonny," she assured him, and picking up her bag of magazines, she started for the door, pausing on the threshold to brush the dust off her long black dress and to adjust her hat. "I am going up one side of town and down the other and sell these *Signs of the Times*. You stay right here and I will be back pretty soon with something to eat."

Undaunted and determined she set down the unknown streets of the little town that slumbered beside the railroad tracks. When she returned an hour or two later, true to her word she had a loaf of bread, some cheese, and a sack of cookies for a special treat.

That night they stayed in a hotel and the next morning she went out again to earn enough for the tickets to Weatherford. This time she knew she must go further into the town so she took Ross with her as she herself had no sense of direction and was afraid she might get lost in a strange town. She knew she could rely on her son, who never got turned around.

All morning she worked selling magazines and earned just enough to get them to Weatherford. Since they would arrive there at nightfall and would not be able to start out for the ranch until morning, she knew they would have to get a room there, but she did not worry for she knew her father would meet them and would have cash with him.

Just at dusk the train pulled into the station and Elias Day was there, but he appeared nervous and edgy and his first question was, "Do you have any money, Minnie? I had nine dollars, but I got robbed in the wagon yard where I stayed last night."

The two stared at each other in dismay as they realized their plight. The rest of the way was by team and wagon, thirty miles of rugged trail, and it was now night.

"Where can we go?" Minnie asked, glancing at the shed that served as depot and the prairie all around being swallowed up by darkness. "Where will we sleep?"

"I guess we can go down to the wagon yard where the team is.

We can sleep in the hay there,'' Elias replied.

''Sleep there with those robbers?''

''They can't rob us anymore. They picked me clean last night. We will have to go there. There is no place else.''

That night they went without supper, but Mr. Day had some nuts and crackers which Minnie divided among the children. They gobbled the scanty crumbs like little birds, drank some water, then lay down in the hay. The thought came to Minnie that the Saviour had been born in a place something like this, and she went to sleep thinking that He knew all about such a bed.

The next morning Minnie found a few coins in her satchel that she had overlooked and bought some crackers for the children and a cup of coffee for her father before they started the long, hard, jolting journey across the prairie in the flat-bed wagon. That lumbering vehicle was the only thing that moved across the sea of grass rippling in the morning breeze like waves. The grass parted before them and closed in their wake. The only sound was the creaking of the wagon as the silence, almost palpable, pressed down from a high domed sky.

About noon they arrived at Arapaho where they got their first glimpse of Indians who lounged about the unpainted clapboard store. Anna was afraid and clung to her mother's skirts and Ross and Lewis watched them from a distance. Jimmy, however, always friendly, curious, and even a little brash, tried to talk to them, but they only stared at him, stoic and unmoved. Approaching closer and pointing a finger at them, he yelled, ''Hey, Ma, they can't talk.''

At that one of the biggest men there, a huge brown man with straight, black hair falling to his shoulders, got up from his post on top of a barrel, and with a quick movement, grabbed the grinning boy by the collar and led him squirming, red of face and frightened, back to his wagon. After depositing Jimmy in front of his mother, he turned without a word and strode with great dignity back to the empty keg where he sat down, folded his arms, and once again stared off into space. Minnie watched the little drama in terror, as she knew nothing about Indians except stories that she had heard, stories of uprisings and savagery and scalpings. Giving Jimmy a weak shake, she hustled him back into the wagon, too frightened to scold him.

Once out of Arapaho, the team and wagon became nothing more than a mere dot on the plains, swallowed up by the boundless range and sky. They passed a scattering of homesteads with people living in dugouts, sod houses, or forlorn and gray shacks. For hours the wagon jolted along the faint trail going east. Elias had been watching the sun and studying the horizon all around for some time, and seeing nothing change, pulled the team to a halt, stepped down from the wagon, and looked around. "Minnie," he said at last, "I believe we are lost."

"Lost," she repeated, "lost," and the very word itself echoed like a dismal bell. Turning slowly around, she could not see a tree or a rock for a reference point. Earth and sky flowed on and on with no beginning and no ending.

Losing heart then, Minnie slumped against the wagon wheel and sobbed. The children clung to her and cried and in the gathering darkness she remembered one black night in Wyoming when she had walked back to Higby amid the howl of wolves. Then she heard it—the same wild, menacing howl rising and falling through the still, vast expanse of night. "Wolves, Pa, wolves! Oh what are we going to do now?" and she grasped the children and looked wildly about.

Elias stiffened as the howls undulated across the miles from some point back behind the thickening night. Holding up a warning hand he listened, mouth slightly open as if to absorb the sound with his whole being. Then he heaved a sigh of relief and faced Minnie. "Relax, all of you. That's not wolves. Those are hounds, and I know where they are. Now I can get my bearings and we will be home soon."

CHAPTER

12

The Drought

The new house that Logan and Elias had built jutted out of the prairie, windows reflecting the last rays of the setting sun like a beacon on the edge of some sea. Other women must make do with dugouts or sod houses, small, cramped, and airless, but Logan had spared nothing for his wife, even adding a pleasant reading room, knowing how she liked to study.

The Sypes were all set up for farming. Besides three milk cows and their calves, two of them heifers, they had a fine team of horses, a flock of hens, and some ducks. A variety of household goods, farming implements, and buggies completed their worldly goods.

Things seemed to be going well, but still when Minnie awoke in the dark hours before dawn, a time when nibbling little worries come out like mice, she felt alone and far away and longed for the home she had left. She thought of herself as one of her apple trees, plain and round and rooted deep in the soil of Iowa, uprooted now and set down in arid rock. Some other force had unearthed her. Some other plan greater than hers had taken over. She thought of the text "All things work together for good to them who love the Lord," wanting to believe it.

Summer gave way to fall and in the thin sunshine the winds sighed through the prairie grasses and on dark days keened, mournful and far away. Minnie stopped her work at that distant murmur, threatened by its sadness. Still, looking out over the farm, she nourished a sort of contentment. Her summer garden had flourished, and she had canned and dried food for winter. The wheat had been harvested and the corn was maturing, the dry leaves rattling in the wind and the silk turning brown at the end of the ear. "Logan," she said at the close of one long and satisfying day during harvest, "I reckon I'd be glad to live here until the Lord comes."

The days grew shorter and the nights became cool enough for a fire in the stove. Winter drew on, and while it was not the long, harsh winter of Iowa, it was, nevertheless, winter.

Even a practical person like Minnie who loved her home and garden had dreams. That winter while the blizzards raged and when the sun came out to melt the snows that ran downhill in narrow singing rivulets she dreamed and started to make them come true. She was only one person, she reminded herself, but she was one. And even though a woman, her dream was to live God's truth before those who knew nothing about it.

To whom could she witness when only a scattering of houses dotted the three miles of prairie between her and Gyp, the nearest town? A tiny, shabby settlement consisting of a general store, a post office, and a few houses thrown up here and there. Its only tie to anything was its name—Gyp—from the gypsum found in nearby soil and rock. But among those who lived there were Asa and Sarah Crippen.

Logan met Asa Crippen at the store in town while both were purchasing supplies. The two chatted for awhile about farming and crops and soon fell into a deep discussion about the second coming of Christ. Logan, sensing someone searching for spiritual truth, invited Asa and his wife to attend church services the next Sabbath. Since arriving in Oklahoma the Sypes had been holding services at their home, as the nearest church was 13 miles away by horse and buggy down uncertain roads. Logan led the singing and Minnie conducted a Bible study.

Although it was only a small home church it was growing. At first it consisted of just the five of them, but before long another family seven miles away heard about the meetings and drove each week in a lumber wagon, bringing their children and often staying all day. Now the Crippens would enlarge the congregation.

Asa and Sarah Crippen proved to be eager and enthusiastic Bible students and after studying for a few months and attending Sabbath School they were ready to join the church. In the spring, after the water had warmed up, a pastor from the nearest conference office held a baptism in the Washita River.

As Minnie watched the little company grow, it seemed that this was where God wanted her and Logan to work, here in this place, raising their children and doing what they could for those around them, preparing them to meet the Lord.

The spring of 1901 found homesteaders all across the land buoyed up by the hope of a bumper crop. Logan planted acres of corn and wheat and watched closely for the first shoots to break through the soil. Wheat rippled in the breeze, a blush of green in the distance.

Day after day the sun blazed down on the young crop. The corn grew taller and the wheat thickened. When the corn was six inches high, farmers began to talk a little nervously about rain when they met by chance on the road or in the store.

"We need a good shower about now."

"Yeah, a little rain wouldn't hurt none."

"Oh, you know how it does out here—always rains just in time."

"Not always—remember a few years back—"

"Crops look great, but if it doesn't rain soon—" and the voice trailed off as the farmer squinted up into the unclouded sky.

Every morning the sun rose in a cloudless sky and every evening it went down in a golden haze of dust. One night just at dusk, clouds formed in the west and spread across the sky. Minnie and Logan, walking out through the field where the corn stood dark green, thought they heard rain beginning with a light patter like mice feet far back in the field, tiny feet scampering over the ground, approaching closer and closer. Before they saw it they felt it on their faces like a coolness. But only a few drops fell and then the wind brushed the clouds away and once again the innocent blue sky curved over them.

In July a hot wind blew up and continued day after day. That Sabbath the little group worshiping at the Sypes had special prayer for rain. On Sunday the rest of the churches prayed, but it did not rain. Some talked about getting the Indians from the reservation to do a rain dance.

The wind continued for three days, burning the crops to a crisp. There would be no yield that year at all. By August not a spear of grass remained in the pastures, and farmers found themselves forced to feed the cows and horses precious hay and grain they had planned to save for seed or for feed during the winter. All Logan had for his horses was broom corn seed and kaffir corn. Unaccustomed to such strange fare they ate it only when starved to it. They grew thin and gaunt, their ribs standing out and their long patient faces looking even longer. He watched his team fattened on Iowa hay and oats turn into skeletons, and by spring he had to sell them for fifty dollars.

The cows grew hoarse bawling for food day and night, the hollow, mournful note echoing across the plains. They gave less and less milk until their udders shriveled up. The best milk cow, old Buttercup, disappeared, and when Logan found her back in the far pasture, she was dead and wolves had gnawed on her carcass. One by one the calves died and then the other cows.

They had nothing to feed the chickens, and the fowl ran listlessly after insects, but for the most part they sat gasping in the heat with their wings extended. The wolves began to prey on them until only a few remained. Those lived only because they grew wild and roosted high in trees and were wary of anything that moved. The ducks, with no water, fared even worse.

With nothing to burn but cow chips, the big house looming up on the prairie was cold that winter. The howling wind reached in with icy fingers and Minnie closed off all but the kitchen. Coal had to be shipped in, and since the railroad was 35 miles away, it was an impossible distance to haul it even if they had money to buy it with.

The great drought of 1901 spared no one. Ranchers and farmers saw their hopes dashed as they had to sell off first one thing and then another in order to exist. The horses, the good buggy, the wagons—all were sacrificed. Stock dead, everything sold that could be sold, there was nothing left.

When she no longer had any garden to tend or cows to milk, Minnie took her bag of tracts and visited her neighbors. She found many in despair, but pointed out to them the Heavenly Hope. As she visited and prayed with her distressed neighbors who were trying to hold out and prove up their claim in the face of disaster, she found herself on the eve of an adventure that would change the course of her life.

C H A P T E R

13

The Lady Preacher

The bone-dry summer of 1901 prompted some to pack up what they had left and move back east, but stubborn hope kept many there. Next year would be better.

Minnie visited her neighbors, and, after the experience of the drought, a number showed an interest in the Gospel and in the news of the coming of the Lord that they would not otherwise have had. A church in Gyp asked her to speak about the Bible on Sunday morning after Sunday School. People from other churches in the area heard about her talks and often asked her and Logan and the children to come and spend the day with them. It was not unusual for her to give one Bible study after Sunday School and another in the afternoon.

A few of the neighbors began to observe the Sabbath, and the small gathering that met in the Sype home grew until it became necessary to find roomier quarters in the school house. By spring a church was ready for organization at Gyp. The president of the Oklahoma Conference arrived in response to Minnie's letter to form the Gyp Seventh-day Adventist Church, later called the Butler church.

One Sabbath after services at Gyp, Brother Williams stopped her and said, "Did you know they's a couple of Advent families over by Putnam? I heard they hold church in one of the homes."

"I'll have to get over there and visit them," she replied.

Early in the week she and Logan drove to Putnam and found the two families who were trying to keep the Sabbath. They, in turn, knew others in that area who were searching for Biblical truth, so Minnie stayed busy for weeks giving studies in various homes. After a few months a church organized at Putnam. In addition, Minnie and Logan eventually formed several companies.

All of her evangelistic activity in the country would have been impossible without Old Jim, the horse loaned to them by the members of the Gyp church. Unlike the fine team they had brought from Iowa that couldn't survive under drought conditions, Old Jim was a native Oklahoma horse, strong and wiry, used to toughing it out on burnt grass and kaffir corn. Ewe-necked and cowhocked, he was anything but pretty, but he could trot for miles, pulling the buggy up and down those dusty trails in the heat of summer and the cold of winter.

Her success did not go unnoticed in the Oklahoma Conference office. As the reports came in of a church here and a company there, as the little tithe checks arrived and the offerings, small but steady, dribbled in, the conference leadership began to wonder and to talk about it among themselves. "Brother Sype is doing a good work out there in Butler County," one commented.

"Not Brother Sype, but Sister Sype," another informed him.

"What! A woman preaching and raising up churches? You mean to say they are going to let a woman preach?"

"*Let* her preach! There is no stopping her!"

"Where did she come from?"

"Some little place in Iowa. She and her husband are homesteaders, but now, of course, with the drought—"

"What is her training, her educational background?"

"Normal training school someplace. She has been a teacher."

"The way she is going maybe we should all go home and send out our wives," an administrator chuckled.

"Amazing, isn't it? Well, she has done a lot of work. The least we can do is send her a check. I'm sure she can use it."

The check for twenty-five dollars arrived in the mail as a complete surprise to Minnie and Logan, but a few weeks later something even more unexpected happened. A stranger pulled up to the gate in a livery stable buggy and announced that he was from the Oklahoma Conference and wanted to see Minnie Sype. She ran up from the barn rather taken aback at the sight of the tall, dignified man who appeared even taller in his black suit and top hat.

Was this the evangelistic dynamo of the frontier, he wondered, *this round, plain, little woman who seemed shy and ill at ease?*

"I am Minnie Sype," she said, the direct brown eyes meeting and holding his. "What can I do for you?"

He came to the point of his visit at once, for he wanted to get back to the depot in time to catch a return train. "The Oklahoma Conference wants you to work for them, Sister Sype."

"I am working," she reminded him. "I work several hours almost every day among the poor homesteaders out here."

"I know you work, Sister, and we are grateful, and more than a little amazed at what you have done. But now we want you for a regular worker. You will be on the payroll and get a check every month for doing just what you are already doing."

She promised she would talk it over with her husband and let him know. When Logan arrived home he was as surprised as she had been. "There isn't much left here on the farm for us," he reminded her.

"Nothing, you might say, with the team gone, the last cow dead a long time ago," she replied. "All that is left of our stock are those few chickens that hide out like wild things and lay their eggs wherever they please."

"Don't forget the ducks," he reminded her with a wry grin.

"Oh, yes, those poor ducks that are alive only because the children watch them and put them into that little box at night." Minnie stared at the floor for a long time before saying, "I just don't know, Logan. I really don't think I can take on a job like that, not having any training and all."

Then he helped her make the decision to accept the offer by declaring firmly, "Mamma, if you go into this work, I will stand by you and do what I can. I will sing and open the meetings, and you can tell the people the Truth."

Nodding, she commented, "It does seem to be the call of God from the way things have worked out, the way things have happened. Even my sister, Myrtle, coming out just now to help us. She will be able to take care of the children when we go out calling. It does seem as if this is what we are supposed to do."

Sometimes life hands one a script, expects him or her to learn the lines, and then to step out onto the stage and not fail. So it seemed to her as she stood on the threshold of a career that she had not trained for and had not planned on, but somehow seemed to be falling into.

The new conference evangelistic team that now ventured forth consisted of Minnie the preacher, Logan the singer, and Old Jim the horse. Often it was necessary to add Ross, as Minnie had no sense of direction, and when she made her visits without Logan, as she often did, she had her son, who was 11 years old then, drive the horse for her.

At that time the Sypes spelled their name Syp, though pronounced with a long vowel sound. Inevitably when Ross and Minnie drove up to a church, they would hear murmurs here and there if not shouts of, "Here comes Sister Syp from Gyp," using the short "y." Sometimes small boys would chant, "Mrs. Syp from Gyp."

It irritated Ross who implored his mother, "Can't we do something? I don't want to be called 'Sip.' "

"I have told them how to pronounce it, sonny. I don't know what else to do."

"I have it, Mother. We can change the spelling. If we put an 'e' on the end, everyone will know it is Sype."

From that day on they spelled their name with an "e."

One of Minnie's first official calls came from the Ruth church 13 miles down the road. As she set forth alone, Logan cautioned her to stay on the main road so she wouldn't get lost. She disliked going by herself as she feared nothing as much as getting lost. Invariably she would turn the wrong way and had gotten lost in town, in buildings, and many times on country roads. She well knew the panic that came from searching in vain for some familiar barn or rock or tree, the frustration of turning back, the futility of retracing her steps, of starting out in another direction only to find that she was still lost.

This time she arrived without incident, pulling up to Brother Stoop's place. Stoop was fixing fence near the house and came running over as soon as she stopped. He was a short, stocky farmer, red of face and ever in motion. Because he was hard of hearing he always shouted. Helping Minnie down from the buggy, he bellowed, "Howdy, glad to see you, Sister Sype. The missus says you have to stay all night with us after prayer meeting."

"I appreciate that. Old Jim doesn't mind going home after dark, but I can't say I fancy it."

He took the horse's head and fiddled with the bridle and then turned to Minnie, saying in a voice that one could have heard in the next county, "I want you to speak on a certain subject tonight."

"What subject is that?"

"The law of God. I want you to speak to us on the law of God."

"I can't do that. I'm not a preacher. I just came to help out in a Bible study for prayer meeting."

"But you must," he exclaimed, his red face growing even redder. "Some of our people are getting discouraged. The preacher who has been here has been trying to tear down the law, and we want you to explain this subject."

As he stood there blinking against the sun, pleading with her, she could not say no. "If that is what the Lord wants me to do, I don't want to refuse, but I'm afraid I can't do it justice."

"I'm sure you can," he boomed. "Tell you what, I am just going to put Frankie on a horse and let him go around and tell the neighbors, and I want you ready to talk on that subject. Here, I'll put your horse up for you." He disappeared into the barn with Old Jim, stopping once to shout over his shoulder, "The law of God, mind you."

"The law of God," she mused. "I'll have to give this some study." She saw the shadows lengthening as the afternoon wore away. "I have to be alone—ah, there—" and she spied a canyon behind the Stoop house.

There she went to study and pray and prepare her message. The burden for witnessing rested upon her, but she didn't feel adequate to perform the task she was being called upon to do. Yet who else was there to do it? Sitting down on a rock she outlined her talk, and that night spoke to a full house.

As she brought out Bible truths she could see the wonder grow on the faces of the people. They asked her to come back in two weeks and speak on another subject. She spent those two weeks studying long hours to prepare for her next homily, and when she returned she found a large crowd waiting.

After the meeting a young woman with a sweet, shy smile came up to shake hands, saying as she did so, "I enjoyed your sermon so much, Sister Sype. It was just what I needed."

Later after everyone had gone, the thought struck her that the young lady had said "your sermon." Requests came from near and far after that for her to hold meetings, and people began to call her the "lady preacher." The term bothered her, as she had no intention of preaching. She disliked women preachers and could not see herself in that role. Suddenly the situation and all that it meant began to overwhelm her. Thinking about the opposition, public criticism, and public opinion that she would have to meet, she knelt in prayer and cried out, "Oh, Lord, I never can do this."

But then, in the midst of her tears there came an impression so strong she knew it was from God, "My Grace is sufficient." She got up from her knees determined to do whatever God wanted and to leave the result with Him. Let them call her what they would, she would not refuse the call of God.

C H A P T E R

14

A Beginning

Mr. and Mrs. Nelson lived in Dewey County to the north of Custer County and the Sype homestead. Struggling wheat farmers near the town of Putnam, they had a dream of their own, a dream of sharing their faith. They asked for Minnie and Logan to hold meetings in the local school house and invited them to stay at their house.

Leaving the children with Myrtle, Logan and Minnie set out early one morning with everything they would need for an extended stay. After a long, hot drive made worse by an unrelenting wind, they were relieved late in the day to see the Nelson's little spread up ahead. They had driven past one poor place after another and this was as unpromising as any. Unprotected by any trees, it lay where the road curved to the left, a few corrals and outbuildings and a tiny house sitting there like some temporary blot on the landscape.

Brother Nelson came rushing up from the barn at their arrival, and his wife hurried out of the house. Children seemed to pop out of the ground. The family lined up in front of the house, watching their visitors. All of them were slight with a thatch of wheat-colored hair and pale blue eyes that stared in stark wonder out of hunger-pinched faces.

Everything there, the buildings, the fences, even the people themselves looked as if the sun and wind and rain had leached the color out. What remained was a spare quality, faded and lean, with all of the fat gone and nothing left but some wiry strength.

"Oh, I do hope you will stay," Sister Nelson said in her soft drawl. "We need to hear preaching and singing out here." She looked around shyly, apologetically, with a sort of desperation.

That night the Nelsons offered the Sypes the only bed, while they rolled up in blankets all over the floor. Seeing no place to change, Minnie and her husband just pulled the blanket up over them and slept in their clothes. Minnie didn't know what to do with her books, so she slipped them into a little niche between the bed and the wall. The next morning everyone had milk and molasses and mush for breakfast, the standard fare.

Minnie and Logan planned to spend the day driving around the countryside visiting with the ranchers and their families, leaving tracts, and inviting everyone to come. They stopped first to see Al King, the school director, and engage the local schoolhouse for that evening. The raw-boned, weather-beaten rancher who looked as if he never removed his hat or his boots regarded them reflectively before drawling, "Shore, you can have the schoolhouse for your meetin's. Welcome to it, but I don't reckon you'll need it long."

"Oh, yes we will," Minnie insisted, "we'll be here a couple of weeks or longer."

"You don't understand, Ma'am. These folks is the roughest set of people I've ever come across." He fixed his penetrating gaze on her, his eyes the color of storm clouds. "Why, they run out every preacher that comes here. And they've never even heard of a woman preacher! They shoot revolvers around the school. And they sit in the back of the room and play cards while the preacher gives the sermon. You can't do nothing with them. The worst of all is them boys from the Rocking R. I tell you, Ma'am, when they get liquored up, they's no telling what they will do. They are a bad lot," and he shook his head mournfully.

"Bad lot, huh?" Logan repeated. "What do you say, Minnie? Shall we go ahead?"

"Absolutely. God surely sent us here, and He will give us strength to bring the message to these people. I thank you for the warning, Mr. King, but God will take care of those men."

Still shaking his head, the rancher watched them drive off. In spite of his warnings they had a pleasant day visiting and found many interested in the Bible. Late in the afternoon they came to a log corral where a group of cowboys stood around in animated discussion. While the couple watched from the buggy, one of the men walked over to a horse that was saddled up and tied to a snubbing post. He seemed different from the others somehow, better dressed and with something of the air of a dude about him. The rest called him Mr. Harvey respectfully enough, but with a tinge of mockery in the way they addressed him.

Harvey sauntered over to the bronco and with a quick, graceful leap landed in the saddle. The horse gave a slight shudder and sank down a little, gathering himself like a runner on starter's blocks, and then he exploded, whirling, bucking, and snorting with his ears pinned back and the white showing in his eyes. His rider lost a stirrup, grabbed for the saddlehorn, slipped to one side, then flew out of the saddle to land with a thud along the fence.

The sight produced a great deal of hearty knee-slapping laughter among the men, but no one ran over to help him. Ignored, he lay where he fell while the laughter continued and money passed from hand to hand. Bruised and battered, Mr. Harvey at last got to his feet, found his hat, and not even dusting it off, jammed it on his head. He limped over to his own horse and rode away without a backward glance.

Minnie turned to a short, bandy-legged cowboy who was still convulsed with laughter and asked, "What is so funny about seeing someone get hurt?"

There was a boyishness about the weathered and lined face, and the cowboy moved and talked with a quick eagerness. "You see, Ma'am, you're new around here, ain't you? Well, you see, this here stranger just rode into camp and let us know he was one wrangler who had never been throwed. And you see, Ma'am, we got this here little horse that has never been rode. So it seemed only fair that the two of them should meet—" After going off into a fresh peal of laughter, he introduced himself as Hank McCoy, foreman of the Rocking R Ranch.

"What can I do for you?" he asked politely while his visitors exchanged glances.

"We are Logan and Minnie Sype," Logan said, shaking hands.

"Oh, you are the lady preacher," Hank McCoy exclaimed. "We've heard of you. Say, boys," he shouted, interrupting the lively conversations over by the corral, "this here is Minnie Sype, the lady preacher. And this is Logan Sype, the singing master. Now if you boys was to go to her meetings instead of the Gold Nugget Saloon, it might do you more good."

Turning back to her he repeated, "The lady preacher! Say, you just wait till my missus hears you are here. She's great on religion, my missus is. Wants to come and hear you speak."

Turning toward the house, he yelled, "Libby, Lib," and getting no response, said to a small boy standing near the fence, "Billy, run up and tell your ma they's someone here she'll want to meet."

At once a small, strong Oklahoma woman rushed out of the house, tying her sunbonnet on as she ran. Her eyes were brown and untroubled and her face round and fair. "Lib," her husband said, "this is Minnie and Logan Sype, the preachers we been hearing about."

"Sister," she said with a hug for Minnie, "we are surely sisters in His name."

Later as they drove away Logan remarked dourly to his wife, "Well, we've met the Rocking R boys."

"Yes, but we've met Libby McCoy, too."

The night of the first meeting the couple arrived at the schoolhouse early to prepare for the meeting. The Nelsons soon rattled up in a lumber wagon with all of the children. After a long wait they heard a clatter of hooves outside and they all tensed, expecting the Rocking R boys, but three young men from a neighboring ranch entered the room, boots echoing against the floor.

When no one else came, Logan opened up the service with a song, and Minnie gave the sermon she had prepared. Part way through the meeting a light drizzle began to fall, and before they had finished the last hymn, the rain poured down. When they started to leave they looked out at a wall of water that made travel impossible. Hour after hour it continued. The little group in the schoolhouse, too tired to talk, milled about or tried to get some sleep on the floor. Finally the downpour lessened and at 4:00 a.m. let up enough so they could go home.

The next day when Minnie went to the store, the storekeeper said, "No offense, Mrs. Sype, but where are you folks sleeping over at the Nelsons? I know they don't have much room." He then invited them to his home as he had a spare bedroom where she could study in peace and quiet.

The Sypes spent their days making calls and nights preaching in that schoolhouse chapel. The trickle of people increased until crowds began to attend. Some were interested in the topic, which was a systematic study of the prophecies, some were curious to hear a woman preach, and some merely wanted to have something to do.

But they came in such numbers to hear the lady preacher that the schoolhouse had standing room only. As it grew warmer, they opened the windows wide and people sat around outside in their buggies and listened under the sky. Neither rain nor harvest stopped their attendance.

Remembering the warnings of Al King, the Sypes listened for the sound of galloping horses, shooting, and drunken shouts, but night after night all remained quiet. Not one shot was fired, not one threat made. Of course, Libby McCoy was there most nights with her rich contralto voice and warm smile, often accompanied by Hank who never ceased to look uncomfortable and out of place in church. But the infamous cowboys from the Rocking R went elsewhere for their fun.

The little evangelistic team traveled around Dewey County the rest of the summer and winter and the next summer. As a result of their efforts churches organized at Putnam and Tologa. At camp meeting the second summer, Minnie received a ministerial license, largely, she suspected, because of the conference president who gave her encouragement and support and was not opposed to women preachers.

CHAPTER 15

Enid, Oklahoma

All things work together for good to them that love God'' was a promise that Minnie had clung to during the time of drought when the cows died one by one and the crops dried up. The hardships had led her into the ministry. Because of the drought she had begun to preach and had received her ministerial license. She had raised up churches where there had been none before. The evangelistic series she had just concluded in Meno had resulted in 32 baptisms.

One day a land speculator came along and agreed to trade them two houses and two lots in Enid, Oklahoma, for their homestead. So now in the summer of 1904 they moved to Enid where Minnie became pastor of the Seventh-day Adventist church and Logan the assistant pastor.

Minnie unpacked her dishes and set them in the cupboard and arranged the furniture. They were now homeowners and, indeed, landlords, for they rented out the second house. Life settled into a pleasant rut with the children attending church school in Enid. Minnie held meetings, visited, and gave Bible studies, Logan helping when he could although his health continued to give him problems.

The conference wanted Minnie to hold a major evangelistic series in the area. Of the two choices for a location, the little town of Carrier or the city of Enid, Minnie favored Carrier, a small country town. She had spent most of her life in the country, and it was among rural people that she felt most at home.

After church she met together with the board members and

explained the situation to them. "We must decide today if we go to Carrier for the series of meetings or remain in Enid. I am going to leave the question for you to decide."

They discussed the matter for some time until at last old Mr. Jacobson pulled a gold watch out of his pocket and stared reflectively at it. "Time is getting away from us," he remarked. "You know what they sometimes did when they had a problem they couldn't solve in Bible times—they cast lots."

"Well, brethren, what about it," Minnie asked. "Shall we cast lots and see where it falls?"

They all agreed to the idea, and after kneeling in prayer, they cast lots and it fell in favor of Enid. The effort began in Enid during the annual Week of Prayer and continued all winter.

While out visiting, Minnie discovered much interest in the meetings but many had no way to get to the church. After the members had discussed the problem at prayer meeting one evening, Brother Thompson assured them, "That is no problem. Brother Butka and I have talked this over. We live out in the country and have plenty of horses, so we can send our families to church in buggies and then each of us will take a big wagon and go through town gathering up the folks that can't walk to church."

"And another thing," Brother Butka added, "you know we both have sisters living in town, so they can go out during the day and invite people. Then they can let us know who needs a ride." It was such help that made the meetings a success, resulting in 40 new members.

James Sype died early that spring. When the telegram came from his mother, Logan knew he must go to her. He went alone, taking gifts from the children to their grandmother, a little vase from Anna and a lace handkerchief from Jimmy.

On the long train trip to Iowa he grappled with his thoughts and feelings about his father. When he saw his father lying there, he wept silently though his whole heart longed to weep aloud and cling to his father.

When he returned to Enid some vital spark seemed to have left him, as if in spite of his own resentments his father had given him some of his strength, and now he had nothing to draw on.

CHAPTER

16

The Return to Iowa

Minnie didn't realize how homesick she had been for Iowa until she began packing to go back. Awash with memories, both sweet and bitter, she could not work fast enough getting ready for the trip.

The opportunity to return had come unexpectedly, and she and Logan both seized it. Logan had begun to think the climate or something in the air itself or in the water aggravated his lung condition. By this time Oklahoma had lost all enchantment for him, and he dreamed of other places where his health and strength would return.

His wife, who had enjoyed a strong constitution and good health all of her life, now began having digestive problems since they had moved to an area of Oklahoma where the water was loaded with gypsum. Spells of vomiting left her weak, and when the doctor could find no other cause, he advised a change of locale.

As the two of them debated what to do next, a request came for Minnie to serve in Iowa as the conference evangelist. The years in Oklahoma had been good to Minnie. Here she had done what few women had accomplished. The time had been right and she had overcome prejudice and participated in the spiritual growth of the frontier. But she always thought of herself as an Iowan, and deep inside, so did Logan. It seemed to both that God was leading them back to their home state.

Rain fell that May day in 1906 when the family left Oklahoma, a cold, gray, unpitying rain. The church members came down to the depot as a group to see them off. Huddled under umbrellas they sang, "God be with you 'til we meet again," and shouted "goodbye," the roar of the train drowning out the sound so that the Sypes saw only open mouths and waving hands.

The train pulled into Creston, Iowa, on a bright spring day. A cold, blue sky curved above the brown weeds that winter had left to rattle stiffly in the breeze. An enduring sameness comforted them. Returning to Iowa was like opening an old familiar gate that creaked its homey welcome.

After five years' absence they had a lot of family news to catch up on. Long quiet talks followed that first excited rush of togetherness, the shouted greetings, the hugs and kisses. Minnie and Logan's first assignment in Iowa was at Lorimar to assist the young minister holding meetings there. A number were baptized at their conclusion.

A few nights before the baptism, one of the candidates waited until everyone had left. The rumpled little man, who came alone and spoke to no one, shyly approached Minnie. "Begging your pardon, Ma'am," he said, crumpling his cap in his hands and looking down at his own boots, "I wonder if I could have a word with you?"

"Yes, of course, what can I do for you?"

Shifting his weight from one foot to the other, he stammered, "Well, you see, I aim to get baptized tomorrow and well, there is something I just got to make right."

"Something is troubling you?"

"I have been doing wrong," he replied, glancing around and lowering his voice. "It's something terrible—shameful. Now I have quit doing it, but I have to confess to the one I have wronged."

Wondering what dangerous criminal confronted her, Minnie took a step back from the shabby, troubled little man who pressed closer and closer to her. For the first time he looked up, the pale stricken eyes seeking her face. "I am a thief," he whispered, "I have stole from my neighbor. I have been stealing eggs from Zack Wilson, my neighbor."

Shaken by his own confession, he had trouble with his voice, but managed to go on, "I've got to straighten things out before I'm baptized, so I am going over there tonight and tell Zack. I've taken a heap o' eggs so I suppose it will cost me some—likely more than I can pay off right away, but I am going to get it off my conscience." With that he jammed his hat on his head and left.

The next night he returned, this time jubilant as Zach had refused to take any money for the stolen eggs. "Said he wouldn't take a cent, not a cent. Said he believed I must be in earnest or I wouldn't be willing to confess my sin like that."

That fall Logan stayed in Afton to take care of his mother in her last illness. It had become increasingly difficult for him to help with the meetings, as his asthmatic condition made him short of breath. His energies flagged and it grew impossible for him to lead the singing.

Both boys had enrolled at Stuart Academy near Des Moines so Minnie now lived with Anna in Cedar Rapids. The girl was a great comfort to her. She loved her boys but their adventurous approach to life worried her. She especially felt concern about James who wanted to make money and to have fun above all else, unlike Ross who had his life already mapped out and persevered in the direction of his goals.

James was charming and attractive to girls, and they flocked around him, but he had no ambition for an education and seemed to be content working from day to day, spending what he earned. His happy-go-lucky nature sometimes got him into trouble. Afterwards he would be contrite and resolve to do better and affirm that he would become a Christian.

Minnie prayed much about all of the children but especially James. If she awoke in the night her worries stalked her in the darkness and sleep refused to return. Where was he tonight?

When Minnie went to Stuart Academy to visit the boys, the administration often asked her to speak. On one of her visits Prof. Floyd Bralliar, the principal, said, "Sister Sype, I wish you would conduct a series of chapels for the students and insist on pure, straight living for them."

The next morning she presented a talk that started a revival. Classes did not meet after chapel, for the students met in prayer groups to confess their sins and get right with God. She gave an altar call at the next meetings. Tears were shed, sins forsaken, and old grudges forgotten. Many committed themselves to Christ, but James did not join them.

When she packed to leave the next day, he came to her room, and sitting down beside her, took her hand and said, "Mamma, I wish I could be good. I wish I wouldn't give in to temptation—like the other night when I was out after hours and got caught coming in. I wish I wouldn't do such things becausc I know it disgraces you and hurts your work.

"But I don't think I am cut out for school," he continued. "I am going to drop out at the end of the term and get a job in Cedar Rapids, to see if things straighten out."

It was something that they had talked about before and argued over from every angle. Now Minnie remained silent, having nothing more to say.

She knew what it was to stand before crowds of young people and feel them yield to her words, to see them change as a butterfly emerges from the cocoon, wet and weak and uncertain but beautiful. At those times she felt a kind of power. But now she felt none of that. Here with her son she felt a great helplessness. She stroked his dark head and wept.

CHAPTER 17

Selling Magazines

When she bought the tickets from Stuart Academy to Des Moines, Minnie found she had only a few cents left in her pocketbook, not enough to get her and Anna the rest of the way home to Cedar Rapids. She had spent more on clothes for Ross and James than she planned.

Impractical about managing money, in the past she had depended upon Logan, but now she often had to face such problems by herself. She knew, however, from experience, that given a few books and magazines to sell, she could travel anywhere and earn money as she went. Now she planned to sell magazines in Des Moines while they waited for the next train.

Once on the coach, Anna curled up and slept while Minnie settled back and watched the passage of familiar scenery, her thoughts dwelling not on her financial situation but on the revival at Stuart with the students coming forward one by one to give their hearts to the Lord. Seeing in her mind the faces of those who walked down the aisle, she remembered also the individuals who sat stubbornly back in their seats, among them her son.

Anna had a bad cold when they left Stuart, and by the time the train reached Des Moines she had the red cheeks and glassy eyes of a child with a high temperature. When she cried it was with the strident voice of croup.

Minnie sat down on one of the benches in the depot, the child hot and limp in her arms. The grime of years of travel had been ground into the floor of the stuffy, crowded room, rank with cigar smoke. Worn and weary travelers huddled over their luggage and milled aimlessly around.

I can't leave my child here, she thought, *and she is too sick to follow me about while I sell magazines. And I must get money for the tickets.* Her eyes roamed around the room and then through the window she saw a building across the street. People came and left it in a steady stream, and something told her to go there.

Picking the little girl up, heavy now in her deep sleep, she crossed the street. Once inside the building, she found it in sharp contrast to the depot, for here it was clean and cool, and although busy with many walking in and out, it was quiet.

She took her coat off to make a pallet in a corner for Anna to lie on and then went around selling papers to the men and women passing through the high domed rooms. Working until almost train time, she felt a satisfying weight in her purse, surely enough to buy tickets to Waterloo where they would change trains for Cedar Rapids.

Arriving in Waterloo at midnight she was thankful that she had $.50 left in her purse so she could get a bed in a hotel for her sick child. She carried the little girl out of the big, echoing, drafty depot to a nearby hotel. Anna didn't wake up as Minnie put her to bed, but slept on, her rasping cough cutting through the deep silence of the night.

In the hotel room Minnie sat down heavily by Anna's bed, wondering what to do next. After paying for her room she had not one cent left. The morning train departed at 7:00 a.m. so there would be no time to sell magazines to earn the fare from Waterloo to Cedar Rapids. She had an appointment at Cedar Rapids in the morning that she had to make and which she would miss if she took a later train. Her mind going in circles, she poured out her problem to God.

At once the answer came. In her bag of papers she had a book, one copy of *Christ's Object Lessons,* which she had stuck in at the last minute. Springing to her feet she rummaged through her bag until she found it.

To whom could she sell a book at one o'clock in the morning while the city slept? Easing through the door, she crept down the long dimly lit hallway leading to the lobby. No one sat there in the circle of worn leather chairs, no late arriving salesmen, no one waiting for a train. Only the heavy silence of a big room desolate at 1:00 a.m.

Glancing about she stood for a moment holding the book to her, and then she saw him, the night clerk slumped behind the desk, neither asleep nor awake. He didn't see her until she cleared her throat and said with a cheerfulness that she didn't feel, "Good evening, or is it good morning?'' her voice breaking into his reverie.

Startled into consciousness, he asked sleepily, ''Can I help you?''

''Yes, you can,'' Minnie replied, stepping forward confidently. ''I have a wonderful book here about the greatest Man who ever lived and some of His timely lessons for us. You'll never get a better bargain for a dollar.'' She thumped the book down before him.

The desk clerk reached out sluggishly and leafed through the volume, a frown deepening in his sallow face. ''I don't think so,'' he said as he pushed it back to her. ''I get all the material I have time to read from my own church.''

''I'm sure your church provides you with inspirational reading, but you don't want to limit your reading to one source, especially when you can secure a book that you will find as helpful to your Christian life as this book will be.''

''No, I'm really not interested,'' and he shook his head firmly.

Finally Minnie burst out in desperation, ''Mister, I must tell you, I have a sick girl upstairs, and I must catch the seven o'clock train in the morning in order to make an important appointment. I spent my last cent on our hotel room, and now I am without money. I thought if I could sell this book I would have enough to buy our tickets to Cedar Rapids.'' She turned wearily away, adding, ''I don't know what I am going to do now.''

''Now wait,'' the hotel clerk said kindly, ''if that is the reason you want to sell the book, I'll be glad to lend you the money you need.'' He pulled a dollar from his billfold and pressed it into her hands.

Minnie held the sick child in her arms on the train ride to Cedar Rapids. At the depot she called her friend Emma Bloom who took them home in a closed carriage. There Minnie treated Anna's croup with a good warm bath, hot teas, and rest in her own bed.

While traveling Minnie always carried a supply of magazines and sold them on the train, in the depot, or if time allowed, out on the streets. In that way she earned money while she witnessed.

Back when she had been working in Oklahoma she received an urgent telegram one day to come over to a nearby cattle town to help two men holding tent meetings. They faced opposition from another denomination that had pitched their own tent nearby and were doing all they could to upstage the Adventists. As a last resort they put out posters advertising that they would feature a woman evangelist and ten singers.

Immediately Minnie had boarded a train in response to the desperate telegram. As it happened, the other denomination did not produce a lady evangelist or ten singers, but Minnie gave the Seventh-day Adventist effort a substantial boost, and on the way she had a singular experience.

It was a warm, airless day, and after hurrying to catch the train, Minnie plopped down in the nearest seat and sat fanning herself and trying to catch her breath. Her bag of magazines lay at her feet, and when the conductor came to take her ticket, she said, "Now I have something for you."

Swaying slightly with the motion of the train, he looked down at her warily and said, "Yes?" Then he steadied himself with a hand on one of the seats as she went into her sales talk, staring at a spot over her head and not really listening. She finished with, "And all of this good reading for only 10 cents, one dime," and pushed the magazine into his hand.

With a shrug he muttered, "Oh, all right," and fished around in his pocket for a dime and took the magazine.

The train made many stops as it was also a way-freight. At one small town it sat on a siding for a long time. When the conductor passed by again, Minnie asked, "How long before we leave here?"

"Hard to say. We have to wait for another train to pass us. You'll have time for a good nap."

Patting the bag at her feet, she said, "If we are going to be here for an hour, I want to get out and sell magazines. Is it all right if I go up town?"

"Go ahead. It will be at least an hour. I'll find you before we leave."

Soon one could see a short, round, black-clad woman bobbing up and down the streets around the depot. When it was time for the train to leave, the conductor came for her. He stopped in the shade of a building and waved at her from across the street. Finishing up a sale, she hurried over.

The heat had settled down heavy and oppressive. Nobody moved very fast—nobody, that is, except Minnie, who appeared to be stimulated by it. "You seem to be doing all right," the conductor said, wiping his brow.

"Yes, I am doing just fine. Time to go, is it?"

"Just about, but I want you to sell one of those papers to the station agent. I'll pull up to the station to pick you up. I have spent an hour reading your magazine, and I can say it is the best I have ever read."

The station agent turned out to be a man looking for religious truth. Minnie stopped there many times as she traveled and the man was always waiting for more periodicals. They had many talks while she waited for the train, and one day when she stopped he was gone. She found out that he no longer worked for the railroad but had quit after becoming a Seventh-day Adventist and was now selling magazines himself.

The first time Minnie took her magazine ministry into a saloon was in Sheridan, Wyoming, where she and the two little boys had gone to do some shopping. As usual she took her bag of magazines with her, and after she finished the shopping, she found a shady place for the boys to eat lunch and look at some picture books she had for them while she went along the street with her publications.

Before she started she sat down on a bench and folded her plump hands in her ample lap and bowed her head in prayer. "Oh Lord, be with me today. Help me as I go about this work. Give me strength to enter every house to which I come. May Your Name be glorified. Amen."

She went from one house to another not knowing the street contained a saloon, but when she left the fourth house and started for the next one, a familiar sour smell hung in the air, and she saw the building was a saloon. With hesitant steps she walked up to the door, paused, turned back, and then remembering her vow to enter every house, pushed open the door. All eyes focused on the matronly woman who marched up to the bar. The loud talking and laughing stopped, and men lingering over their beer or playing cards watched in surprise. She was not the kind of woman usually seen in a saloon, not someone who looked like your mother.

Stopping first before a man lounging near the bar, she asked him if he would like to buy a magazine. "I never buy from common peddlers," he growled, shifting his cigar from one side of his mouth to the other.

"Better a common peddler from God than a peddler for the devil," she retorted and turned to the bartender, a red-faced man polishing glasses behind the bar. "How about you, mister?" she asked, "only ten cents for good Christian reading."

He leafed through the magazine and then slid two dimes across the bar. "I'll take two," he said and handed the other paper to the man with the cigar. "Here, Julius, this might do you some good." Gathering up her courage, she sold several more before closing the heavy door behind her with a sigh of relief and continuing on down the street.

CHAPTER

18

Ellen White

After Logan buried his mother early in the spring of 1909, he again joined Minnie in evangelism. He hoped that the rest he had gotten while taking care of his sick mother would enable him to help now, but his asthma and emphysema soon worsened and he found it almost impossible to lead song service or even to walk very far.

Since he could not assist her anymore, he stayed home most days and tried to have something ready to eat when Minnie returned so she would be refreshed for the evening meeting. Late in April on a cold drizzly day Minnie arrived home to a cold house and no sign of a meal. Her temper flared and she yelled, "Logan, isn't supper ready? The meeting is due to start in an hour and I must have something to eat."

Hearing a noise from the bedroom she went in and found him in bed, scarcely able to breathe. "Oh Minnie," he gasped, "this is it. I am going to have to give up the work."

"Oh, no, you will be better in a week or two. This spell will pass," she assured him.

Shaking his head he said with a sad firmness, "No, it only gets worse. I'll send in my resignation as your assistant. I can't do the work anymore, and it is wrong for me to take a check from the conference." Slipping into a wracking cough, he lay back on the bed, weak and pale.

"But Logan, I need you."

"I haven't been much help to you for a long time, Mamma."

"What am I going to do without you?"

"You will do what you have always done, preach the word, get the truth out to the people."

Minnie went on with her work alone then, and Logan retired to the farm in South Dakota operated by Minnie's sister Myrtle and her husband Walter Manful.

The Iowa camp meeting that summer of 1909 was a special one to which Minnie looked forward, for Mrs. E. G. White was scheduled to be one of the speakers. Ellen White had guided the Seventh-day Adventist Church from its infancy and was becoming a legend in the denomination.

Except for James, who never could sit through long meetings, the family would be together. Logan joined his wife and Anna, and Ross, who was on the reception committee, met them at the depot. He bustled around putting their trunk into the dray, showing them to the buggy that would take them out to the camp grounds, and being generally helpful.

"They keeping you busy, son?" his father asked.

"Sure are. A big crowd is expected this week. Sister White is going to be here, you know."

"Has she come yet?"

"No, she's due on the six o'clock train. You wouldn't believe the preparation that's going on around here. Her room has everything anyone would need. There's a cot by the platform in case she tires, and there will be at least one aide for each service to help her up on the platform."

"Are you one?" Anna questioned excitedly.

Ross smiled down at his little sister. "'Fraid not. I only have the honor of seeing that her luggage reaches her room safely."

After escorting them to their tent, Ross said, "Do you know that Mrs. White will speak at the workers' meeting in the morning at 9 o'clock? I know you won't want to miss that." He paused, smiling broadly, before adding, "I have more news."

"Well, what is it?" Minnie asked impatiently. "Come on, out with it, I know that grin."

"Gertrude Hunt and I are engaged."

"A sister for me," Anna squealed. "And Gertrude is so pretty. I love the name Gertrude. You know I asked Aunt Myrtle to name her baby Gertrude."

"I've always liked that girl," Minnie said, nodding slowly. "Pretty but no nonsense."

"When is the big day, son?" his father questioned.

"Not right away. We're both going to finish school before we get married. She is still in nurses' training, you know, and I want to graduate from college first. Well, have to go now." Ross glanced at his watch. "Work is waiting. See you at the meeting tonight. Gertrude will be there and wants to see you, too," and with his wide, irrepressible look of joy, he sprinted away between the tents.

Crowds had come from great distances to hear the prophet of the Lord, and Minnie and Logan arrived at the meeting early that night in order to get seats well up to the front of the auditorium. During the song service the participating ministers filed up onto the platform, and then a little wave of excitement rustled through the congregation as Ellen White entered. She had never been in robust health and now in her eighty-second year appeared small and weak as she leaned heavily on the arm of her aide and tottered across the dais to her seat.

"She doesn't look like she'll make it through the meeting," Logan whispered.

"I'm glad we got a front seat so we'll be able to hear her," his wife whispered back.

Anyone there at the Iowa camp meeting that evening never forgot hearing Ellen White speak. She rose unsteadily to her feet, and, assisted by her aide, shuffled over to the podium and braced herself by holding on with both hands. Before speaking she stood quietly, her eyes roving over the assembled crowd. Not a sound disturbed the silence. Even the children were still as every ear strained to hear her as she began to speak in a thin, thready voice.

Although beginning softly, almost inaudibly, she grew stronger as she spoke until her strength returned and her voice vibrated to the tent top. How could such volume come from that small, delicate woman with an almost transparent frailty? Releasing her hold on the pulpit, she walked freely on the rostrum as she exhorted those present to cleanse their lives from sin and prepare for the glorious coming of the Lord.

The next morning Minnie and Logan went to workers' meeting where Ellen White had pertinent counsel for all. After the benediction, when they began filing out, Minnie heard someone call, "Sister Sypc."

Puzzled, she turned and found herself face to face with the prophet of the Lord who smiled pleasantly and took her hand and chatted for a few moments about the family. Then she said, "Sister

Sype, I have heard about the good work you are doing. Keep it up. The Lord is pleased with your success."

Discussing it with Logan later, Minnie said, "Why, it was just like talking to anyone. She was so encouraging and understanding. It was like a sign, her talking with me."

"It was a sign, Minnie. You must never give up the work. Never."

CHAPTER

19

James

The call from Jesse Samuels came a few days before Thanksgiving. It was one of those November days when low clouds hunkered over withered fields and the whole world seemed in mourning. Minnie had met the Samuels in Humbolt, Iowa, but they had moved away. One of their little girls had died and they wanted to return to Humbolt to the family home for the funeral and burial. Brother Samuels begged Minnie to go with them and conduct the service.

They traveled together on the train back to Humbolt, a long, sad trip with the tiny coffin in the baggage car. Minnie conducted the funeral in the Humbolt church, then went with the procession to the cemetery. Dark horses pulled the hearse, and leaves scampered across the cold, stiff earth. In the cemetery, the trees stood stark and black. Finally the bitter service came to an end.

Minnie caught a late-night train home, and when it stopped at the Cedar Rapids depot it was early morning, Thanksgiving Day. She walked the few blocks to the house. Though the sky was leaden and the air damp, holiday spirit hung in bright wreaths from doors and clustered in carriages around different houses.

But she felt none of the holiday joy—only a great crushing weariness of body and mind. Exhausted from the funeral, the grief, and the long train ride, she told James and her husband who had come home for the long weekend, "I don't want to see anyone or talk or eat. I just want to sit here and rock for a spell."

She had no more settled down and taken off her hat and shoes when the phone rang. Logan answered it. Minnie closed her eyes and tried to calm her troubled mind. As she rocked back and forth, the motion and squeak of the chair soothed her. When she heard her husband's footsteps, she did not look up. "I'm sorry, Mamma," he said after a pause. "That was Sister Johnson. Brother Johnson is very low and she needs someone."

"Oh," she groaned, "I was afraid of this. Typhoid. Someone has to go out there." She reached for her shoes.

James stood up and touched the back of her chair. "Mamma, let me go out there and help Mrs. Johnson. I'm off work tonight and I know how tired you are. You stay here and attend the potluck dinner the Ladies Society is getting ready."

"Bless you, son, I do need a little rest. They will be sewing on comforters and writing missionary letters this afternoon. That will be relaxing compared to the last few days."

Just before she went to bed she called Mrs. Johnson. The woman's husband had not gotten any better. "I'll come out first thing in the morning," Minnie promised.

She had just dropped into a deep sleep when the harsh jangling of the telephone woke her up. It was James. "Mamma, Mr. Johnson is just hanging on by a thread. I'm afraid if you wait 'til morning, it will be too late."

"I'll catch the next trolley," she told him.

James met her at the end of the line with a buggy and they drove through the cold, foggy night. The patient's breath was ragged, his lips blue. Although Mrs. Johnson was a dedicated Christian, her husband had never given his heart to the Lord. Minnie took his thin hand and talked to him about his salvation, reading the twenty-third Psalm. "Mr. Johnson, don't you want to become a Christian?" she asked.

"Mrs. Sype, if I live, I will be a Christian."

"My brother, you are a very sick man. You may not live to keep your promise. Remember the thief on the cross who accepted Jesus when he was facing death? Don't you want to follow his example?"

The dying man's lips barely moved. "Yes, pray for me. I want God to forgive my sins."

They all knelt around his bed and Minnie committed him to God. Mr. Johnson's lips fluttered briefly, but they heard no sound. Then he was quiet.

James had never seen death before and it visibly shook him as his mother pulled the sheet up over the face of the man who had talked just moments before. Completely overcome, he sat with his head in his hands until Minnie led him into the next room where he fell on the couch in a troubled sleep.

The next day he went up to his mother, put his arms around her, and said, "Mamma, there is no life worth living but the Christian life. I am tired of the world and sin. I want to turn my life around."

On Sabbath, she asked, "James, aren't you going to church with us?"

"No, not today. Everyone will think I am there just because Mr. Johnson died. But I'll go with you next Sabbath, I promise."

One evening before leaving for work, he entered the kitchen where Minnie and Anna were preparing supper. He handed his mother two dollars and said, "Here is the money I borrowed from you." Then he gave his sister some change and dropped a quarter on the table in front of Minnie.

"Money I get that way goes into my mission box," she said.

"I should have known," he laughed. "Well, it's no great sacrifice." He teased the two until Anna pushed a piece of pie across the table.

"You and your jokes," the girl laughed.

Charm was both James' blessing and his curse, clinging to him no matter where he went. It wasn't anything he even said or did. A big, handsome young man, the hint of a smile shone through his eyes and around the corners of his mouth. Inevitably, people felt drawn to him. When he entered a lagging party or sat down at a table, people came alive.

Thursday evening Minnie came home from a busy day. For a moment she thought of calling her son, but realized that the train had just arrived and he would be busy at his job meeting hotel guests. Feeling relaxed and happy, thankful that he had decided to return to church, she went on to bed.

The shrill ringing of the telephone pierced through her peaceful sleep. She covered her head with her pillow, but it didn't go away. At last her sleep-fogged mind realized that she should answer it, so she stumbled through the dark to the telephone. Suddenly, fear was bitter in her mouth.

"Do you have a boy working at the Allison Hotel?" asked a strange voice.

"Yes, my son James."

"He's been badly hurt."

Minnie held on to the wall. "Bring him home at once."

"I'm afraid that will not be possible. They have taken him to the hospital. You'd better come."

Minnie and Logan found their son unconscious. They stood by his bedside and she took his hand and stroked his hair. Bowing her head, she prayed, "Oh, Lord, surely You will not let my boy die without saying something to his mother."

The doctors came in and worked over him. At last he began to stir. Moaning, he opened his eyes. One hand touched his ear. "What is the matter with my ear? Did I get hit by a train?"

"No, James, you got hurt," his father said.

"Who hurt me? I wasn't fighting."

"No, you weren't fighting, but someone hit you," Minnie explained.

"Did they put him in jail?"

"Yes."

"Save the papers for me to read." Then he lapsed into another coma.

Some of the men who had been there told Minnie just what happened. After finishing up his tasks at the hotel, James had decided to pass the railway station to see how the porters under his charge were getting along. It was almost time for a big passenger train to arrive.

He saw a one-armed drayman who had a reputation for being a troublemaking drunk pushing one of his boys around. Hurrying forward, James ordered him off the platform. The man wheeled around to face him. Waving the hand with the iron hook, he sneered, "Who's going to make me?"

"You know the porters from the hotels are the only ones allowed here. Now get out or I will call the police." The drunk scuttled away, muttering curses and threats.

At another station, James paused to see if the Milwaukee train was on time. Unknown to him, the angry man had followed him in the darkness. He crept silently out of the shadows and when James turned his back, the drunken drayman struck him on the back of the head with his iron arm hook. James dropped without a sound and men came running from the station to rush him to the hospital. The befuddled drayman stood blinking in the light of the lanterns and the police soon hustled him off to jail.

Friday dragged by with James slipping in and out of a coma. On Saturday doctors moved him to a private room and he seemed to get better. He was happy that Ross had come to see him. "Hello, kid," he said weakly. Although he was three years younger, he always called his brother "kid," with a kind of mock deference. "They got me this time, kid. Right on my hard head."

Ross took his hand. "We're praying for you. I know you're going to be all right."

"Sure, kid," James said with a wry smile. He turned to his mother. "Mamma, what day is it?"

"It is Sabbath, James."

"And I was going to church with you today. I didn't get any further than the hospital." He passed his hand wearily over his head. "When I get out of here, I'll go with you every week."

He seemed to be stronger, and seeing his improvement, Minnie went home that night to get some rest. At three a.m. she awoke drenched in sweat, her heart beating wildly. She had fought her way out of a dream where James was lying in an open coffin on a hill someplace. It was dark and dank with fog swirling about. Out of the fog came six crows, flying in twos. Hearing their harsh caw, she had awakened and stumbled to the phone.

The nurse at the hospital said James was restless. Letting Logan sleep as he had been having a bad time with his emphysema, Minnie woke Anna and they dressed to go to the hospital two miles away. They paused at the door to stare out at a cold, driving rain, but there was nothing else to do but go out in the downpour and wait for the streetcar. Standing in the numbing cold, they felt like the last two people on earth. But even more terrible was the icy fear that James was dead.

As soon as they entered the hospital room, they knew he was worse.

"Mamma, is that you?" he asked weakly.

"Yes, son. Anna and I are both here. We'll stay with you." She gave him a kiss on the cheek.

"Mamma, close the door and pray for me." His voice was urgent, frightening.

Kneeling together in the hospital room with its cold, grim hospital smells and distant night sounds, they prayed. While the rain beat against the windows in the darkness of pre-dawn, Minnie prayed, then Anna, and finally James. James prayed again, as men have ever done when pain is all-consuming and death approaches.

He struggled to focus his eyes on his mother's face and touched her hand lightly. "It's all right, Mamma. If God sees best not to heal me, I'm ready."

Those were his last words. He died later that day, December 10, 1911.

Numb with grief, Minnie knelt alone and begged God to help her arrange an appropriate funeral for her son. Earlier that year a fire had destroyed much of their personal property and set them back financially. She and Logan had no funds with which to bury their son.

At last, Minnie went to the funeral director and told him of their financial condition. "What am I to do?" she asked. "I don't have any money but I must have my boy laid away respectably."

He assured her with Christian charity that it would be done. Going home she helped ready the front room for James' return. He would be carried into the room, his merry eyes closed, his smiling face stiff and cold. She looked around the quiet room. *My poor boy, I cannot buy you flowers. You will have to be laid away without them.* It seemed more than she could bear.

But flowers began to come. Even before they brought James' body home, wreaths and bouquets arrived. In the end, they covered the coffin and people flocked to the house to offer sympathy and sit with the family. *To think James knew so many people,* she thought. In a small way, it brought comfort. But it was only when she thought of the resurrection that despair turned to hope.

CHAPTER

20

On the Train

In the evening when the dark pines sobbed against the lemon-yellow west like lost children, Minnie thought of her loved ones, gone from her now. One by one those nearest and dearest had left until she was all alone. Her father had to her surprise and joy joined the Seventh-day Adventist Church, but he had died a few months afterwards.

Logan caught a heavy cold from which he made no improvement in Iowa, so the doctor suggested he go where the air was drier. Minnie's sister, Myrtle, and her husband were living in Canada then, and they thought that might be the place for him, so he packed up to go, following another will-o'-the-wisp that might lead to health and healing.

In her heart Minnie wanted to go with him, but they both knew she must stay where her job was. Still financially strapped, she did not even have money for her husband's trip to Canada, so she borrowed from a friend. When she took Logan down to the depot he gasped for breath even though he walked slowly, dragging one foot behind the other.

"Not like I used to walk, is it, Mamma?" he wheezed as they waited for the train. "Remember how fast I used to walk?"

"I remember. I was always begging you to slow down for me."

The porter had to help him up the steps, and as the train pulled away, she watched the thin, gray face in the window disappear from sight, wondering if she would ever see him alive again.

With Anna away at school and Ross married, she had made the

last break with her family, and when she returned to her apartment from the depot and faced the empty rooms, a rush of loneliness swept over her.

Praying for strength to rise above her losses, she threw her energies into her work which became her only satisfaction.

She served as Home Missionary Secretary of the Iowa Conference now and traveled up and down the state, becoming known as Mrs. Home Missionary. In her work she helped young people sell magazines and encouraged the churches to implement the Harvest Ingathering program which she had supported since first hearing Jasper Wayne speak in 1907. Here she was in her element, as she often said she would rather try to get ten people to work than to do the work of ten people.

At this time she felt impressed to do a book on her life and experiences, and although she found writing a chore, she kept at it night after night. In 1913 her *Life Sketches and Experiences in Missionary Work* came off the press. Numerous friends had preordered the book, and by filling the requests she managed to meet some pressing financial obligations.

So the days and weeks passed and became months and years. Anna married and moved to her own home, and Ross and Gertrude sailed for Central America. She still thought of James with a grief undimmed by time. Iowa was full of sad memories for her now, and when she returned home after being away on a trip, the past flitted ghostlike through the quiet rooms.

With nothing to hold her in the state anymore she quickly accepted a job offer from the Washington Conference. Elder A. R. Ogden, who had transferred there from Iowa and knew of Minnie's abilities, wanted her to serve as his Home Missionary Secretary. Making the position more attractive was the fact that Anna and her husband had decided to move out there.

On a fall morning with the early sun flickering through the trees to the east, Minnie boarded the train for the West. Slowed now by age and arthritis she climbed stiffly up the steep iron steps of the railroad car, clutching in one hand the bag of papers she carried with her on trips. She settled into a seat and reminiscences of Iowa flitted through her mind.

The early morning sounds of people in the streets outside the station reached her, but an intense loneliness filled her, and she remembered the loneliness of other days.

Once on a street in Waterloo a man had stopped her and asked, "Pardon me, but are you a Christian?" and when she said she was, he begged with a desperation like that of the last man on earth, "Pray for me." Then he disappeared into the crowd. Minnie now knew how he felt.

She recalled crowds and faces and long rides on trains and in buggies with the cold wind blowing or the hot sun high above. They rolled on—the memories—afternoons in dim parlors, small gatherings in tiny houses back behind hills, as well as huge congregations where long lighted halls led to an auditorium seating hundreds.

Filled with her own thoughts, Minnie turned away from the slowly filling day coach and fixed her attention on the scene outside where the engine huffed and puffed like some great animal gathering strength for the journey. Above its rhythmic panting she felt rather than heard the wind rising far off with a low sound like rain. Distant trees writhed with it, but in the enclosed space between the depot and the train no air stirred.

Going West—a beginning, she thought, *and an ending*. But she knew that with the Christian hope of Christ there were no endings, only beginnings that transcend all meanings. She closed her eyes and thought again of James and of Logan and Anna and of Ross far away.

She pressed her head against the cool window pane, and it was when she looked up that she saw the butterflies—monarchs gathered for their ancient migration. There was no counting them as they fluttered uncertainly past the window of the train in the slate-gray light of the early morning, heading west as was the train.

Going West like me, she thought.

For a long time she watched them, wave after wave of butterflies, delicately beating the air with their deceptively fragile wings—all headed resolutely west.

Epilogue

Minnie labored in the Pacific Northwest for 11 years, serving as Home Missionary Secretary of two conferences and pastor of several churches. (Two of those years she spent in the East as Circulation Manager of the *Watchman* magazine, later *These Times*, and as pastor of a church in Pennsylvania.) While in Washington State, Logan died. Five years later she married Ben Atteberry. Soon after that she retired and they moved to Florida, where they remained for 13 years until Ben passed away.

Minnie then went to live with Anna in Portland, Oregon. It was while there that Asa Crippen, her convert from her Gyp, Oklahoma, days, re-entered her life. His wife, Sarah, had died and he had heard that Minnie was widowed. They renewed their friendship and married, both of them nearing their eightieth birthday. After Asa's death two years later, Minnie returned to Portland, where she died in 1956 at the age of 87.